# Games for Thinking

# Games for Thinking

## ROBERT FISHER

Nash Pollock
Publishing

First published in 1997 by
Nash Pollock Publishing
32 Warwick Street
Oxford OX4 1SX

9 8 7 6 5 4 3 2

*Orders to:*
9 Carlton Close
Grove
Wantage
Oxfordshire  OX12 0PU

A catalogue record of this book is available from the British Library.

ISBN 1 898255 13 X

Typeset in 11.5 on 14.5pt Cheltenham.

Design, typesetting and production management by
Can Do Design, Buckingham

Printed in Great Britain by Redwood Books, Trowbridge

# Contents

# Introduction

*Avoid compulsion and let early education be a manner of amusement. Young children learn by games; compulsory education cannot remain in the soul*

Plato

*I don't learn much by playing, but I learn a lot through thinking*

Jane, aged 8

Play is the central activity of childhood and it comes in a myriad of forms. At its best play provides children with activity, enjoyment, co-operation, discussion, investigation and problem solving. Through play children can experience 'the joy of being the cause'. Through play children can learn things they would not learn in any other way. The whole of human culture, it has been argued, derives from our capacity for play. Perhaps a better explanation is that human culture derives from a capacity to think about and learn from our creative activity, and this activity includes playing games.

The essence of a game is that it involves actions undertaken for the purpose of enjoyment. But games can also have serious purposes. They can help us to practise skills, to develop concepts and strategies. At its most mundane play can become a succession of repetitive and mindless routines. Perhaps as a result of this, playing games other than sports in school has largely been seen as something for young children or as spare-time activity. The job of the teacher is to see that educational play has purpose and structure – that it is not merely filling-in time. Without the help of a teacher or mediator setting the environment and providing suggestions, children's play often reaches stalemate and becomes intellectually aimless. The aim of this book is to provide a collection of games for children, students or adults to play and to think about. Each game is followed by extension activities and questions to challenge and extend thinking about the game.

*Games for Thinking* contains over 100 games that can be played by individuals, small groups or classes , at home or school, to help develop skills in thinking, and learning, logic and language.

The games were designed for use in home or school. They can be used in a variety of ways, for example;

- to enrich teaching and learning within the curriculum, particularly in English and maths
- as a regular 'Games for Thinking' activity, in home, class or club, for example for an hour a week
- as a whole class lesson, for example introducing a new thinking game from time to time
- as an activity for a group while other classroom activities go on
- as extension material for children to read, learn and play for themselves in their own time
- as homework assignments, to involve parents in playing and discussing games with their children
- for use with other children's groups such as parties or play-and-learn sessions

## Why games?

*Games lubricate the body and the mind*                    Benjamin Franklin

*The best things in life are games*                              Tom, aged 9

We have all experienced the enthusiasm generated by games such as chess, cards, Scrabble, Monopoly and so on. Games can generate enthusiasm, excitement and enjoyment. But are games merely an enjoyable interlude from the business of life, or can we use them to teach the skills of living and learning?

The first advantage of using games for thinking is that they can motivate children's interest and activity. In addition games add variety to what is being taught and learnt. Effective teaching involves 'variety in learning activities' (HMI 1990). If one of the characteristics of effective teaching is the use of a range of teaching methods then games can add a variety to the teaching of any subject, providing opportunities for:

- individual work
- work in pairs
- work in small groups
- work in large groups or whole classes.

Games can provide a motivating start to lessons, or round off a period of work in an entertaining and challenging way. Games can also function as the focus of a lesson if they are 'games for thinking', that is games that have both curriculum relevance and cognitive content, by for example encouraging discussion between groups of children and between pupil and teacher.

The success of teaching depends to a large extent on the active involvement of the learner. Children learn by making the concepts, knowledge and skills they are taught their own. Playing games demands involvement. A good game cannot be played passively: it demands co-operation with others to be played effectively, and players must be actively involved if they want to win. Games embody the twin sources of co-operation and competition:

- co-operation with others in sharing in an enjoyable rule-governed activity
- competition with others in seeking to succeed or to win.

All the games in this book rely on the co-operation of players following agreed rules and playing well together to improve their performance or reach a goal. Through shared activity games can help foster a sense of community, of inclusion and cohesion within a group, as well as help develop the social and co-operative skills of individuals. *Games for Thinking* offers an extra co-operative dimension, in the questions for thinking and discussion offered at the end of each game. Games can offer not only cognitive challenge but also opportunities to develop moral understanding and practise social skills.

They can also help develop emotional intelligence, in particular the disposition to think for oneself, and to value the thinking of others. All the games require the co-operation of individuals and groups. They can help develop self-awareness, independence and self-reliance in individual players, as well as co-operation with and respect for others. Playing these games is not just about developing skills, but also the values and positive attitudes needed for sustaining effective social relationships within a community. Examples of personal qualities which can be nurtured through playing these games include: patience, perseverance, confidence, self respect and self-esteem, friendship, trust, honesty, open-mindedness and empathy towards others. Both winning and losing call for the exercise of these virtues.

Games also offer competition with players or groups competing against each other or against some set target to be achieved. The thrill of winning, of achieving a difficult goal, can be one of the most potent of human pleasures – 'to strive, to seek, to find, and not to yield' in the words of Tennyson's *Ulysses*. Children need to develop resilience in the face of challenge alongside other virtues if they are to achieve success in life. Competition between individuals, pairs or groups is motivating if players have real chances of success. We need to find ways of rewarding effort, for example by offering achievable targets such as trying to beat your previous score. As one child commented after playing a game, 'I like playing against myself. It gives me a chance to win.' Some prefer to play in teams, others in pairs or as individuals; so it is good to offer a variety of individual, paired and team games. These games are designed so that players can almost always achieve some measure of success.

Games encourage the active involvement of players, but creating a context for thinking or game-playing will not guarantee that learning occurs. Turning the game into learning means not only showing children how to play the game but helping them to apply creative and critical thinking before, during and after the game. It involves providing cognitive challenge to players through questioning and discussion, so that they become games for thinking as well as for playing.

## What kinds of thinking?

*Good teaching makes clear the importance of application, accuracy and good presentation, and the need to use critical thinking, creativity and imagination.*

(Guidance on the Inspection of Nursery and Primary Schools, Ofsted/HMSO 1995, p68)

*You play better if you think better.*

Paul, aged 10.

'Games for thinking' are designed for children to have fun while exercising their capacities for thinking. The games in this book give players practice in such skills as planning, questioning, reasoning, seeing things from different viewpoints and thinking of new ideas. The following are some of the critical thinking skills which these games help to develop:

- analysing visual and verbal information
- applying rules
- categorising
- checking and correcting
- communicating thoughts and ideas
- comparing and contrasting
- defining and describing
- divergent or lateral thinking
- estimating and educated guessing
- evaluating
- explaining
- forming conceptual links and associations
- formulating questions
- generating ideas and hypotheses
- giving and following directions
- identifying information needed
- logical thinking
- imagining
- making inferences

- making informed judgements
- memorising
- non-verbal communication
- observing
- planning
- predicting
- problem posing
- problem solving, recognising progress towards a solution
- reading for meaning
- seeing another's point of view
- sequencing
- spatial thinking
- strategic thinking
- synthesising
- testing and improving ideas
- understanding cause, effect and probability
- verbal reasoning
- visualisation
- writing and language skills

These games are also designed to help overcome some of the blocks to thinking, especially the three 'intelligence traps' that prevent us from making the most of our thinking – haste, narrowness and lack of focus.

One of the common faults in human thinking is that it is too hasty. We are impulsive and fail to take time to consider alternative plans of action. We do not think ahead to work through the consequences of our decisions, and we do not take time to review and learn from what we have done. We see this in children who respond hastily to moves in a game, who become unthinking 'wood-pushers' in a game of chess. *Games for Thinking* aims to overcome the tendency for haste by emphasising the need to take time to ponder, to puzzle and to think things through.

Another fault in human thinking is that it is too narrow. Through routine and force of habit we become mindless. We become limited to familiar categories and well-worn tracks. We think that there are no choices in getting from A to B, missing the possibility there may be other ways and better ways. *Games for Thinking* encourages players to look for creative options, to consider different viewpoints and ways of thinking about the game.

A third fault is that human thinking often lacks focus. When we lack a plan or strategy our thinking tends to become hazy. If we lack clarity about the targets we need to pursue we become haphazard and overlook what is important. Our thinking becomes random, disconnected and disorganised. We become fuzzy in our approach to problems. *Games for Thinking* encourages a 'planful' and strategic approach that can help make games playing more thoughtful and more skilful.

For example the game 'What if ...?' (p 79) encourages players to create an original hypothesis or variation on everyday thinking that creates a new but possible world, and to consider what the consequences of that hypothesis might be. The 'What if ...?' game is not simply an exercise in make believe. It invites players to extend their thinking by considering the consequences of an imagined situation. 'What if ...?' can be used to develop the four aspects of creative thinking:

- fluency of ideas – how many 'What ifs' can you think of?
- flexibility of ideas – what different 'What ifs' can you think of?
- originality of ideas – what 'What ifs?' are there that nobody has thought of?
- elaboration of ideas – what are the possible consequences of a 'What if?'

Crucially in *Games for Thinking* the thinking is not over once the game has finished. Through questions and discussion players are invited to think carefully, broadly, and purposefully about the game, and to reflect on their thinking through the game (what are the options and consequences?) and beyond the game (what have I learnt from playing the game?) Each game is designed to encourage intellectual enquiry, and to provide opportunities to exercise different aspects of players' intelligence - including the verbal, logical-mathematical, visual, physical, musical, intra-personal and social.

But before playing the game you need to agree the rules.

## Learning the game

*I am still learning*                                    Motto of Michaelangelo

*Before you change the rules you've got to know what they are.*

Gary, aged 8

There are three basic ways for players to learn a game from this book:
1   Let players who do not know the game read the rules together and learn by trial and error how to play.
2   Invite a child who knows the game, or has read the rules, to show others how to play.
3   You explain the game to the players (having learnt the rules yourself!).

There are advantages to be gained from each strategy. If children are puzzling out together how to play a game this has the advantages of co-operative learning, learning from and discussing with each other, sharing an intellectual challenge and more likely succeeding together than if they worked on it alone.

However some children like to puzzle things out by themselves, and if we value independent learning then this should be encouraged. Explaining it yourself is often the quickest way to get into playing the game, provided of course you understand it and have tried it out beforehand. Another way would be to tape instructions for children to follow from the book, with materials to hand, and to store your taped instructions in a games or listening corner. Explaining to children has the advantage that you can monitor their understanding, answer questions and encourage attentive listening.

After the rules and scoring have been understood it is a good idea to play a trial round so that any potential problems or misunderstandings can be ironed out. If any of the rules are difficult to remember they are best copied, or displayed on the wall for all to see. Those who know the rules may be asked to explain the game to others, or to create a poster which advertises and explains the game.

As these games are not just any games, but are Thinking Games, it may be a helpful to explain that the purpose of the game is not just to enjoy playing and to pit your wits against yourself or others, but also to think about and learn something from the game. The aim is to think about the game and how you and others are playing it; and to think about what is going on in your minds while you are playing it, for when you are discussing the game afterwards. So what is it we are hoping the players *are* going to think about, and how do we help them to learn something from the game?

## Questions for thinking

*What then is the right way of living? Life must be lived as a play,*
*playing certain games, making sacrifices, singing and dancing, and then*
*a man will be able to propitiate the gods, and defend himself against his*
*enemies, and win the contest.*

Plato

*Is everything we do just a game?*                                Jane, aged 8

One of the most powerful ways to focus and stimulate thinking is through skilful questioning. Each game in the book contains suggested questions to help extend children's thinking. These questions can be seen to operate on three levels, thinking *about* the game, thinking *in* the game and thinking *through* the game:

1  *Thinking about the game*

   Questions that can be asked about any game include the following

   • Do you think this is an easy or hard game? What makes it easy or hard?

- What other games do you know that are like this game? Can you give examples?
- What kind of game is this? In what category or categories would you put it?
- Is there anything about this game you find puzzling or want to question?
- Do you know the rules? Do they make sense? Are you ready to play?

2   *Thinking in the game*

Questions that could be asked during the play of any game include the following:

- What do you need to do to win, or achieve your target in the game?
- What is stopping you from winning, or achieving your target?
- What strategy or ways of playing will help you in this game?
- What would be a bad strategy or a poor way of playing this game?
- How are you doing? What have you done successfully, and not yet successfully so far?

3   *Thinking through the game*

Questions that can be used in discussion after any game include the following:

- Were you successful in the game? Why, or why not?
- What strategy did you use in playing the game? Was it a good strategy?
- Did you find it an easy or hard game to play? Why?
- Did you think it was a good game to play? Why, or why not?
- What did you think or learn during this game?

With every kind of game in the book there are a number of questions that could form the basis of a discussion to help players come to a shared understanding of the game and of themselves as players. The best questions for discussion might come from the players themselves. One way of facilitating this is through creating a Community of Enquiry.

A Community of Enquiry is achieved when any group of people act co-operatively in the search for understanding. Not only does each member benefit from the ideas and experience of everyone else, each person feels a valued part of the whole community. This structure shares characteristics of effective thinking groups, from political 'think tanks' to university research groups, from industrial research teams to school staffs, from families at home to classes in school. This sense of community has a dual aspect: a *rational structure* for effective thinking and shared ideas, and a *moral structure* of mutual respect and shared values.

A Community of Enquiry approach to *Games for Thinking* includes the following elements:

1 *a community setting:* sit so all can see and hear each other, teacher as part of the group

2 *a game to share:* each has a turn to play, or the option not to play but to watch the game

3 *time to think*: time is given to think before, during and after the game

4 *time to question:* time for raising questions, problems and ideas after the game

5 *discussion and review:* time to discuss questions or comments and to review the game.

During the question and review time after the game each person is given the chance to share any thought, question or comment about the game. These can be written on paper or on a board for all to see. Each has a right and opportunity to express their own opinions and feelings about the game. The name of the person could be written up alongside the question or comment they make, to signify their contribution and ownership of the idea. Everyone should have a chance to share their thinking before discussion takes place. A question or comment is chosen for discussion. The person who made the contribution is invited to explain or add any further thoughts. The subject is then open to discussion by the group.

As in all group discussion it is useful to agree rules for the discussion, for example - 'Only one speaks at a time', 'Everyone listens to the speaker', or 'We each take turns'. It is important that each must listen to others, and consider different views and ideas. Such discussion helps to develop communication skills and self-expression through talking and listening, which can also be extended to writing – for example through a games diary or notebook where ideas can be explored through writing and drawing. What is important is that players have the chance to think about what they have played (What kind of game was it? How would they describe or explain the game to others? What other games is it like?), how they have played (How did they play? What strategy did they use? What is the best way of winning or avoiding losing?) and what they think of the game (What did they think, feel, learn from or about the game?). In thinking about the game players should also being encouraged to think about themselves and about life. In what way(s), if any, is the game they have played like life?

## Extension activities

*Play adorns life, amplifies it and is to that extent a necessity, both for the individual – as a life function – and for society by reason of the meaning it contains, its significance, its expressive value, its spiritual and social associations, in short as a cultural function. The expression of it satisfies all sorts of cultural needs.*

Johan Huizinga

*A good game is like a good lesson, it makes you want to do things.*

Jane, aged 8

Each game section also contains suggestions for extending thinking through activities and exercises that apply and extend the experience of playing the game that has been played. These activities involve players generating ideas for their own version of the game, or playing a variation to compare and contrast. Other extension activities might involve writing, drawing, modelling, measuring, researching, investigating or problem solving.

The games in this book can be used to develop many aspects of intelligence. The first section on Language Games relate to verbal and linguistic intelligence, and include games that help concept-building, definition, memory, questioning, speaking and listening, poetry, storytelling and many other word games. The National Curriculum states that 'pupils' vocabulary should be extended and enriched through activities that focus on words and their meanings, including ... word games' (*English in the National Curriculum* p 12).

The second section, Logical Mathematical Games, relates to logico-mathematical intelligence and includes games that help logical and strategic thinking, and concepts of number, shape and probability. These games are especially useful for developing understanding of 'Using and Applying Mathematics' (AT1) in Mathematics in the National Curriculum. These games give children opportunities to develop mathematical language and reasoning and to develop different mathematical approaches to solving problems.

The third section is a collection of Visual, Spatial and Kinaesthetic games, which focus on drawing, observation, visual memory, miming and problem solving. These can help develop a thinking approach to the expressive arts (art, design, drama and physical education). The games offer models that can be adapted and developed to enrich all areas of the school curriculum, or can be used simply to 'lubricate the mind'.

Each section contains a number of memory games which can be used to strengthen and exercise the memory. Remembering is helped by making patterns out of the information given, and by repeating these patterns until they become internalised into long-term memory. These patterns can be processed in different ways which relate to different aspects of intelligence:

- verbally – through listening and saying or repeating the information
- visually – through seeing a picture or pattern in the 'mind's eye'
- logical mathematically – through seeing a pattern of logical or mathematical relations
- kinaesthetically – through physical representation eg writing, or bodily gesture
- musically – through melody, rhythm or musical association
- personally – through linking the information to a personal experience or story
- socially – through learning with others and remembering a shared experience

The concept of memory is itself problematical. A story with questions for discussion about memory can be found in *Stories for Thinking* pp 74-77, in this series.

What are the benefits of playing games for thinking? There is some evidence to show that when children play these games regularly over the span of a school year that they improve in creative thinking skills and in their ability to participate in group problem-solving activities. Some teachers have reported improvements in verbal reasoning abilities and in mathematical ability, but it is difficult to prove that playing these games will automatically improve thinking and reasoning. It is likely that children will need to play these games over a number of years for there to be real and lasting benefits to their thinking and learning.

But the strongest reason for playing these games is not to improve the players' minds, nor to improve their social skills, but because the games provide pleasure, challenge (including what Yeats called 'the joy of what's difficult') and the joy of exercising one's human capacities in play. And it is a pleasure in which we as adults can share.

Note: For more on ways to develop aspects of intelligence, thinking and learning see *Teaching Children to Think* and *Teaching Children to Learn* by Robert Fisher, published by Stanley Thornes.

# A   Language Games

## 1 Concept games

We make meaning by creating links between words and ideas. We think and learn more by making more links, by exploring and testing links. The following games provide practice and develop skills in making links and conceptual connections.

### Connections

'Only connect', said E.M. Forster. Making connections is the way we create an understanding of the world, and making new connections is the basic process of all creative thinking. Are there any two words or concepts that cannot be linked in the mind through some connecting idea? This game challenges children to make creative connections between words.

*Players*:       Any number, playing individually, in pairs or teams

*Age range*:   Seven to adult

*Materials*:    Display board, pen/pencil and paper

*How to play*

Children play as individuals, in pairs or teams. The aim is to make as many conceptual links as they can between a set of randomly chosen words.

1  Ask children to suggest any interesting word that comes into their heads. Tell them that you want concept words, that is words that stand for something, not connecting words like prepositions, conjunctions or indefinite articles.

2  Display their suggested words, up to a total of 10 or 12 words, on a board for all to see, for example  'head, giraffe, handkerchief, holiday, handbag, balloon, daisy, sun, comic, hats'.

Analyse the answers. Which answer do players think was the most creative. Why?

Play further question and answer games, such as Question games p 38.

Play a variation on Crazy answers, such as 'Random words' p 50.

## Categories

A game in which players must list as many words within given categories as they can within a time limit. The game calls for quick thinking, and verbal fluency.

*Players*:       Any number, playing in pairs or small groups
*Age range*:   Seven to adult
*Materials*:   Pen/pencil and paper

*How to play*

The game can be played individually but is best played in pairs or teams of 3 or 4. Players make a list of 12 or more categories. A target letter is chosen, and players write as many examples of each category beginning with the target letter as they can within a time limit. One point is scored for every category word, and two points if no other player or team has thought of that word. The player or team with most points is the winner.

1   Players begin by each suggesting a number of categories, creating twelve or more in total, for example Animals, Countries, Boy's names, Girl's names, TV programmes, Sports, Book titles, Birds, Clothes, Foods, Towns, Colours. These are listed on a sheet of paper.

2   A letter is chosen at random for example by turning to a page in a book and blindly pointing at a word. This becomes the target letter with which words in every category must begin.

3   Players are given a time limit, eg 15 minutes, in which to write as many words beginning with the target letter in each category as possible.

4   When the time is up each player or team reads out their list of words, scoring one point for each word, and two points for any word not thought of by others.

**5** In each round a new initial letter is chosen. The same categories may be used again or new ones chosen. The player or team with most points wins.

*Questions to think about*
- The game is called 'Categories'. What is a category?
- Which categories in the game were the easiest and hardest to find words for?
- Which initial letter was the easiest or hardest to find words for?
- Did you use any strategy in this game?
- Does every word fit into some category? Can you think of any words that do not fit into any category?
- Do some words fit into more than one category? Can you give examples?
- How many categories of words do you think there are?
- Do you belong to any categories? What categories would you fit into?

*Extension activities*

Brainstorm a list of categories into which everything in the room will fit.

Create a concept map of animal life showing all the main categories of animals.

Devise a database to categorise all the books you have at home or in your classroom.

Collect a large group of objects such as buttons, stones or shells, and classify the collection by dividing them into different categories.

Play a variation on the Category game, for example the game called 'Guggenheim'.

## Guggenheim

*How to play*

Players write a list of categories down the side of a page and a key word, such as the name of a player, at the top of the page. Players must complete a list of words under each letter of the keyword in a given time, say 10 or 15 minutes. The scoring is the same as in Categories. The following is an example from a game:

|  | P | E | T | R | A |
|---|---|---|---|---|---|
| *Boy's names* | Peter | Edward | Thomas | Richard | Alan |
| *Fruit* | Peach | ? | Tangerine | Redcurrants | Apple |
| *Countries* | Poland | Ethiopia | Turkey | Russia | Austria |
| *Birds* | Peacock | Eagle | Tern | Robin | Albatross |
| *Items of clothing* | Pants | Earmuff | Tie | Raincoat | Apron |

# 2  Definition games

The objectives of these word games are to develop expression, comprehension and verbal reasoning, and to encourage players to think carefully about the meanings of words.

## Dictionary Race

It is often difficult to get children to use a dictionary to find or check words. The following is a group of games that involves using dictionaries, and thinking about the meanings of words. The games are best kept short, but played regularly help children gain a familiarity with the use of dictionaries, and introduces them to a range of new words.

*Players*:   Any number, playing as individuals or in group teams

*Age range*:   Seven to adult

*Materials*:   A dictionary for each player or pair of players, pen/pencil and paper (optional)

*How to play*

One way of helping children to become familiar with a dictionary is to have a dictionary race where they are challenged to hunt for words in the shortest possible time.

1   Prepare a list of words, say ten, ready for the players to hunt in their dictionary.

**2** Players each have a dictionary ready for use. A word is called out, and then spelt aloud. Players race to find the word in their dictionaries.

**3** The first player to find the word raises a hand, and gives the page reference and reads the meaning of the word. The winner, or winners, get a point.

**4** At the end of the game the team or individuals with most points win.

An alternative version is to set a target time for teams to find all ten words. Players can create their own lists of words for another team to use in a dictionary race.

Other dictionary search games could involve players finding:
- one letter words, two letter words, three letter words, four letter words etc.
- words that do not include one of the five vowels – a, e, i, o, u
- words that contain two or more vowels in alphabetical order eg 'a' and then 'e'
- words that contain three vowels, four vowels, and then five vowels eg 'facetious'
- words that are compounds eg 'lighthouse' or 'penknife'
- words that are palindromes ie that can be spelt the same forwards and backwards eg 'madam'

*Questions to think about*
- What is the quickest way to find a word in the dictionary?
- Which word(s) did you find easiest or hardest to find? Why was this?
- What use are dictionaries? Who uses dictionaries?
- Which dictionary do you find best to use, or most helpful?
- How are dictionaries compiled? Could you compile a dictionary? What kind of dictionary would be most useful to compile?
- What criteria would you use for judging how good a dictionary is?
- Where do the meanings of words come from? Do the meanings of words ever change? What makes you think so? If they do, how do they change? Can you give examples?

*Extension activities*

Invent other dictionary hunting games, for example finding words with similar endings such as 'ology', or finding words with different derivations such as Greek, Latin, French or Anglo Saxon.

Collect, display and compare different kinds of dictionaries, including dictionaries of foreign languages.

Assess dictionaries for value for money. Compare the number of words in each dictionary with the cost.

Create your own dictionary of words around a theme.

Play race games along similar lines, with other reference books, an encyclopaedia or the Bible.

## Speedword

This game encourages speed of thinking in defining words.

*Players*:       Any number, in groups of 3–5 players

*Age range*:   Seven to adult

*Materials*:   Word lists (see examples below)

*How to play*

The class is divided into small groups or teams of 3–5 players. The aim of the game is for each team to try to be the first to define a given set of words. Begin by offering an example, such as 'It is yellow, round and hot, and shines in the sky'. (Answer: 'The sun').

1   One member of each team is given a list of words which must not be shown to the other members of the team. On a given signal this person has to describe or define each word to the rest of the group who try to guess the word.

2   Each group, playing consecutively, is allowed two minutes in which to guess as many words as possible from their list.

3   The team is awarded one point for each correct answer. No points are awarded if the word itself or a close derivation is used as a clue. The umpire's decision is final.

4   After each team has had a turn a different member of the first team begins the second round by defining another list of words. The following are sample lists of words in ascending order of difficulty:

| List A | List B | List C | List D |
|--------|--------|--------|--------|
| tree | flower | apple | banana |
| car | train | plane | table |
| horse | dog | fish | boat |
| orange | jam | blue | woman |
| boy | girl | man | blue |
| yellow | green | red | oval |
| square | circle | triangle | camel |
| milk | wine | carrot | bed |
| chair | sink | sofa | circus |
| lion | pond | stairs | car |
| fair | house | flat | bucket |
| bus | town | branch | equal |
| library | empty | push | away |
| picture | hotel | trio | |
| football | happy | second | |

| List E | List F | List G | List H |
|--------|--------|--------|--------|
| sprint | couple | elastic | juggle |
| Easter | sadness | family | cliff |
| daughter | shore | private | untidy |
| netball | surround | escape | different |
| bicycle | cupboard | telephone | student |
| factory | video | handkerchief | chemist |
| underwear | garage | wardrobe | jaguar |
| anchor | carnival | earthquake | complete |
| newsagent | rectangle | overturn | excess |
| angry | refuse | contract | microphone |

## Questions to think about

- Do you think this is an easy or hard game? What makes it easy or hard?

- Are some words easier to define than others? Why?

- Can every word be defined?

- How could this game help you in thinking and learning?

- Do words have only one meaning or definition? Can you give an example?

- Who decides on the meaning or definition of a word?

- Can the meaning or definition of a word change? How, or why?

*Extension activities*

What is the record number of definitions a team can achieve in two minutes?

Create your own definitions game, for example using mime for defining words.

Play a definition game with a word limit for the definitions, for example in five words or less.

Research and discuss the definitions different people give of the same word. Are the definitions different? Which definition do you think is best?

## Call my bluff

This traditional game, adapted successfully as a TV quiz, is a useful activity for encouraging creative thinking about the meanings of words.

*Players*:       Any number, playing in groups of three

*Age range*:    Nine to adult

*Materials*:    Pen/pencil and paper, dictionaries

*How to play*

Divide the class into groups of three and give them time to prepare. Their task is to find an obscure word in a dictionary that they think the other groups will not know and create two false definitions. The aim is for other groups to identify from three definitions the correct dictionary definition of a given word.

1   Each group chooses a word from a dictionary and writes the definition down. They then make up two short definitions of the word. When they have three definitions, only one of which is correct, they are ready to play.

2   The word is given for the other groups to see, and the three definitions are read out. The opposing teams have to guess which of the definitions is the correct one. Ingenuity and good acting are needed to bluff your opponents into thinking a false definition is the true one.

3 The opposing teams choose which of the definitions given is correct. If they are right they gain a point. if they are wrong the defining team gain one point for each successful bluff.

Here is an example of a 'call my bluff' definition:

<u>Wedlock</u>

1 A lock for a nineteenth century bicycle.

2 A word meaning being married.

3 The name of a type of lock on the river.

*Questions to think about*

• What does it mean to 'bluff" someone?

• Did you find it easy or hard to make up a definition for a word? Can you give an example?

• Can a word have more than one definition?

• Does every word have more than one definition?

• Have the definitions of words changed over time. Why. or why not?

• Who decides on the true definition of a word?

• Can you think without using words?

*Extension activities*

Make your own Daft Dictionary of invented words with funny or silly definitions.

Compare the definitions of words in two dictionaries. Which dictionary do you think gives the best definitions of words?

Play 'Call my bluff' using famous quotations, ie find a famous quotation and choose three possible people (one being the true one), or a famous person and three quotations (only one quotation being true).

Play some other bluffing games, such as Spoof, p 104.

# 3 Memory games

Memory is the ability to process, store and retrieve information. Success in life depends in part on memory and the ability to recall to mind information that is important. One characteristic of able children is that not only do they remember more about what they are being taught, they also know more about how to remember. One answer that children give to the question 'What helps you to remember?' is 'Practice'. Providing practice on memory tasks and discussing ways of remembering may help children develop more awareness of the mechanisms and strategies of remembering.

The following are some memory games to think about and discuss:

## Suitcase

This is one of a number of games that challenge verbal memory by presenting a fictitious situation where a growing list of items must be remembered.

*Players*:      Any number, playing in pairs, groups or as one large group

*Age range*:    Seven to adult

*Materials*:    None

*How to play*

The players are going on a long journey with a large suitcase. Each player will choose one item to pack in the suitcase, but must remember all the other items already in the suitcase. If a player forgets an item they are out of the game. The player(s) who remembers most items wins the game.

1  The first player chooses the first item to be packed in the suitcase, and tells the others. For example, 'I packed my suitcase with a teddy bear'.

2  The next player repeats these words and adds another item, for example: 'I packed my suitcase with a teddy bear and a bag of crisps'.

3  Each player takes a turn to add something to the suitcase, remembering to repeat all the items that it already contains.

4   Players must listen carefully to each other for if a player forgets any item they are out of the game.

*Questions to think about*

• Was it easy or difficult to remember the items for the suitcase? Why?

• Did you use any strategy to try to remember what went in the suitcase?

• Do you think playing 'Suitcase' could help you to improve your memory?

• How do people remember things? How does memory work?

• What helps you to remember and learn things?

• How could you get better at remembering?

• How do you think memory works?

*Extension activities*

A variation of this game is to pack items for a specific purpose, for example a picnic. Items must be related to the purpose and packable, or they can be challenged by other players and disallowed.

Another variation is Alphabetical Suitcase, where each item must begin with the next letter of the alphabet (allowing 'ex' for 'x').

Can you create your own memory game as a variation on Suitcase?

## Memory

This game also involves trying to commit to memory a numbered list of words.

*Players*:       Any number, good for larger groups

*Age range*:   Seven to adult

*Materials*:    Pen/pencil and paper (optional)

*How to play*

Make a list of ten simple words, numbering them from one to ten.

1   Read the list of ten words with their numbers eg 'One, bicycle; two, lunchbox; three ...' to the group while they listen carefully.

2   After reading the list, say any number from one to ten. The first player to tell you what the word is on the list that corresponds with

the number is the winner and scores a point (alternatively all the group try to write what the word is and all who identify it correctly get a point).

3   After each round repeat the next number, and see how many can remember all the words.

4   After reading all the numbered words on the list, make a new list and start again, this time reading the numbers in random order.

5   Any player can recite, reconstruct or remember the list of words in their original order wins the game (or a lot of points!).

*Questions to think about*

• Have you ever had to memorise a list of words before? Give an example.

• What kinds of people have to memorise words? How do they do it?

• What could help you to memorise a list of words?

• Are there some things that people have said to you that you will always remember? Can you give an example?

• Are there some things you think that everyone should remember? What are they?

• What would help you be better at remembering things?

• Was 'Memory' a good game to play? Why, or why not?

*Extension activities*

Play other memory games, for example the games on pp 88 and 141.

Ask players to devise their own list of words for the 'Memory' game around a particular theme.

Research what others think are the most important ten words in their lives.

Study which are the ten most frequently used words in the English language, for example by recording data from reading books or newspapers.

Keep a Word Book to enter all the most unusual and difficult-to-remember words that you find.

# 4 Poetry games

To write a poem is to play a kind of game with words. If ever we are going to use words to good effect we need practice in playing with them. The following games are some ways of encouraging students to think through poetry about the meanings of words and the ways they can be used in poems. For more on using poetry for thinking see *Poems for Thinking* in this series.

## Scrambled poems

The world is a confusing place. The sorting out of this confusion occurs in the mind. We make sense of the world by conceptualising our experience and putting these concepts into some sort of comprehensible structure and order. Meaning is created by a process of categorisation. We can challenge this meaning-making capacity through scrambling what is ordered and seeing if this order can be restored. The following game challenges players to construct their own meaning and order out of the raw material of lines of poetry. It is an infinitely adaptable, challenging and rewarding game.

*Players*:      Any number, playing in pairs or small groups

*Age range*:   Seven to adult

*Materials*:   Pen/pencil and paper, a poem cut up into lines, couplets or verses

*How to play*

Choose a poem that will interest the players. Reproduce the poem and cut it up into separate lines (if a relatively short poem) or into verses (if a long poem). Have one cut-up poem for each player, pair or team of players.

1   Each player or team of players is given the lines of a cut-up poem which have been jumbled into the wrong order. Their challenge is to reassemble the poem in the order that makes the best sense (and which possibly was the same order as written by the poet).

2   After a given length of time, or when all have finished the task to the best of their ability, the players look at the poems they have created from their given lines.

3   The players are shown the original poem as written by the poet.

The players whose poem is nearest to the order of the original poem wins the game.

The following is an example of a poem with scrambled lines. Can you reconstruct the original poem?

> Take your walk
> Spin and die
> May the little birds pass by you
> To the shady leaf or stalk
> Caterpillar in a hurry
> To live again a butterfly
> Brown and furry
> May no toad spy you

(Christina Rossetti wrote the poem, and it appears in its original form in *Minibeasts* edited by R. Fisher, published by Faber)

*Questions to think about*

- Was it easy or difficult to unscramble the lines of the poem? Why was this?

- Is there only one way the lines of the poem make sense or are there different ways for the lines to be arranged and still make sense?

- Is the meaning of the poem in the words of the poem, or in the mind of the writer or reader?

- Can the same words mean different things to different people? Can you give an example?

- Does a poem or story have the same meaning for the writer and the reader? What is your reason for thinking that?

- Could you put together the lines of a poem in a better order than the poet?

- What did you think or learn while playing this game?

*Extension activities*

Ask the players to choose their own favourite poems to unscramble.

Write the plot of a well known story or play in as few lines as possible, jumble them up and play 'Unscramble a Story'.

Choose a reference book, scramble some lines from one section, play

'Unscramble the Reference Book'.

Copy the pages of a picture book, scramble them up, play 'Unscramble the Picture Book'.

Invent your own unscrambling game eg with recipes, instructions, National Curriculum documents etc.

See also Scrambled Words p 70, Scrambled Sentences p 72.

## The furniture game

This is a guessing game in which a person is described under a number of headings. It is a game that stimulates creativity, verbal fluency and provides good practice in the use of similes and metaphors. The game can be played through speaking or writing as follows.

*Players*:        Any number

*Age range*:    Seven to adult

*Materials*:     Pen/pencil and paper

*How to play*

Demonstrate the game by asking the group to describe someone they know, such as you, under a number of descriptive headings such as : a colour, a season, a place, a type of weather, an article of clothing, a piece of furniture, a TV programme, a food, an animal, a time of day etc.

Ask the group to read out their descriptions beginning 'He is' or 'She is'. Once the group have got the idea the guessing game can start.

1   One person thinks of someone else in the group but doesn't say who it is (and doesn't look at them!).

2   The rest of the group try to work out who it is by asking the sorts of questions suggested above, asking for example: 'What kind of furniture is this person?' 'What kind of pet?' 'What kind of shop?' 'What sort of holiday?' The one who has chosen must answer to give  a clue to who it is.

3   The person who guesses correctly can be the next one to choose to think of someone (or can nominate the next volunteer).

The following is a sample from a 'Furniture game':

This person is crimson red
She is midsummer
A school playground
And a windy day.
She is a multi-coloured duvet
An easy chair
The Big Breakfast Show
A slice of apple pie.

*Questions to think about*

- Were you able to guess the person from the description? Why, or why not?

- How many possible descriptions might there be about any one person?

- Which of the descriptions given about you (or a chosen person) do you think is most accurate in its description? Which do you think is least accurate? Do others agree? Why, or why not?

- Is everyone like a kind of dog, weather, furniture (or other chosen category)?

- Are there some things about a person that are difficult or impossible to describe?

- What is a simile? Can you give examples?

- What is a metaphor? Can you give an example? What is the difference between a simile and a metaphor?

*Extension activities*

Use the game as a writing activity, where each person writes about someone in the group using an agreed range of criteria.

Write about your favourite (or least favourite?) person using your chosen criteria.

Draw a picture of the mystery person, incorporating one or more of your chosen similes or metaphors.

In your group brainstorm as many different possible categories for describing someone as you can.

Can you create a metaphors for something abstract like a feeling (anger, sadness, joy) or to sum up something big like your life?

## Three-in-a-bed poems

Three-in-a-bed refers to the three words that make up each line of the poems in this game. It provides a good introduction to writing poetry for young children and anyone who finds poetry writing difficult. It focuses the mind on the need to observe things closely and to choose words carefully.

*Players*:      Any number, playing individually, in pairs or as a group

*Age range*:   Five to adult

*Materials*:    Pen/pencil and paper, a collection of pictures eg art reproductions, colour magazines or postcards

### How to play

Three-in-a-bed poems have any number of lines consisting of three words. The stimulus for a three-in-a-bed poem can be a theme, such as the street, or a visual stimulus such as a picture. Introduce the game by suggesting a theme or showing a picture. Draw lines or fold a piece of paper to make three columns. Write the names of some of the things connected with the theme, or seen in the picture, in the centre column, as in the example below inspired by a picture by Van Gogh:

| | | |
|---|---|---|
| moon | bright moon | bright moon shining |
| trees | green trees | green trees swaying |
| hills | blue hills | blue hills rolling |
| sky | starry sky | starry sky swirling |
| church | tall church | tall church pointing |
| village | sleepy village | sleepy village dreaming |

In the left hand column write a word (adjective) that describes the thing in the centre column.

In the right hand column put a word (verb) that says what these things are doing. If desired more words may be allowed to be added to any line to help it make more sense.

1   Players are given a stimulus, such as a theme to think about, or picture to observe. Their task is to create three-word-line poems of a given length within a given time, for example a ten line poem in twenty minutes.

2   Each line must contain a noun, an adjective and part of a verb.

**3** At the end of the game the poems are read. Players succeed if they achieve the target of completing a first draft of a poem on the theme or picture.

*Questions to think about*

- How many lines do you think it would be possible to write about this theme (or picture)?

- What was the hardest thing about this game? Why was it hard?

- What did you find easy about it? Why?

- Do (did) you find it better to play with someone else or by yourself? Why?

- What makes a good poem?

- Can you find two good things to say about your poem? Can you find one thing to improve?

- Which was the better (or best) poem? What are your reasons? Who agrees or disagrees with you?

- What do you think or learn in this game?

*Extension activities*

Collect an anthology of poems on a given theme or picture.

Extend the challenge to five line poems, or the writing of cinquains.

What is the longest three-word-line poem that you can write? How much can you think or see in a picture to write about?

## Rhyming tennis

Rhyming tennis is a simple word game which encourages phonemic awareness and quick thinking. With infants it can be played with sounds, with older children with rhyming words. It is called 'tennis' because the rhymes are 'batted' to and fro between individuals, pairs or teams.

*Players*:        Any number, playing as individuals, pairs or teams

*Age range*:    Five to adult

*Materials*:     Pen/pencil and paper, dictionary (optional)

## How to play

Two players or groups take turns to say rhyming words. When a player cannot follow on with a new rhyming word they lose that round of the game. A useful rule is that only words that appear in a dictionary are allowed.

1 A player begins by saying a word, for example 'blue'. The next player or team must say a rhyming word, such as 'flew', the first player says another rhyming word such as 'grew', and the game continues until one of the players cannot say a rhyming word. A rhyming word can only be used once in any game. The player saying the last rhyming word wins a point.

2 The player who loses a round begins the next round with a new word.

3 Play continues until a player wins a set target of points. Any dispute about whether a word is a true rhyme can be settled by reference to a dictionary or to an umpire.

Note: With infants one person suggests a sound and each player in turn offers a rhyming sound. Rhyming sounds need not be actual words. Start with simple sounds at first, such as 'do', 'me' or 'in'. Later try some more elaborate sound combinations such as 'runny, sunny, munny, funny, bunny' or 'halloo, taboo, bongaloo ... etc.' One way to introduce it is to say: 'I want a rhyme in double quick time and the rhyme that I want is ...'

## Questions to think about

- Does every word have a rhyme? (There are very few English words that have no rhyme.) Did you find any words that did not have a rhyming word? What rhymes with 'secret'?

- Many words have only one or two rhymes. Which ones did you find with only one or two rhymes?

- When is it useful to know about rhyming words? Who uses rhyming words?

- Some words which nearly rhyme, such as 'eat' and 'wet' are called *half rhymes*. Can you think of any other half rhymes? 'Beanz meanz Heinz' – what kind of rhyme is that?

- Rhymes must sound alike. Some rhymes are called sight rhymes. They look as if they should rhyme because they end in the same letters, such as 'love' and 'move' but they don't rhyme. Can you think of other sight rhymes?

* People have discovered that if young children are taught a lot of nursery rhymes this helps them in learning to read. Why do you think this might be so?

* Do you prefer poems that rhyme or do not rhyme, or both kinds? What is your favourite poem?

*Extension activities*

Make a collection of your favourite rhymes. Here is one of my favourites, from a tombstone:

> 'Here lies John Bun;
>
> He was killed by a gun.
>
> His name was not Bun but Wood;
>
> But Wood would not rhyme with gun, and Bun would.'

Make a survey of the number of nursery and other rhymes children know.

Find a rhyming dictionary to help you make up some rhymes of your own.

Play 'Mime the rhyme' by miming actions to go with mystery rhyming words.

## Rhyming verse

This rhyming game is a race to complete a four line rhyming verse or quatrain in a given rhyme scheme. It is a challenge to quick thinking and verbal fluency.

*Players*:       Any number, playing as individuals, in pairs or teams

*Age range*:   Seven to adult

*Materials*:    Pen/pencil and paper

*How to play*

Decide on which rhyme scheme to use for a game. The easiest is to use rhyming couplets, that is AABB. Later try quatrains by rhyming alternate lines, as in ABAB.

1   The first player or team gives a word, the second player or team gives a rhyming word. The third player gives the third word, and the fourth the rhyming word. For example:

> Player 1: bright
> Player 2: fight
> Player 3: feet
> Player 4: sheet

2   Players take turns to complete a rhyming verse in couplets using the given rhyming words, for example:

> Fearless Fred was not so bright,
> One day he got caught up in a fight,
> Poor Fred was knocked right off his feet,
> And they had to carry him home in a sheet.

3   The verses are read out at the end, and possibly edited or redrafted! The winning verse could be judged by popular vote.

4   Try playing the game using alternate rhyming lines (ABAB) as in this example:

> Up rode St George in armour bright,
> Which covered him from head to feet,
> Saw a dragon ready to fight,
> But it was only his sister dressed up in a sheet.

*Questions to think about*

•   Do you like some rhyming verses and not others? Why do you like some verses better than others? Can you give examples?

•   What makes for a good rhyming verse?

•   What is your favourite rhyming verse? Why do you like it?

•   Do you find rhymes easy to remember? Why?

•   Are some verses easier to remember than others? Why?

•   Why do you think poets sometimes write in rhymed verse and sometimes write without rhymes?

•   Have you thought or learnt anything by playing this game?

*Extension activities*

Choose, write out and learn your favourite quatrain from a poetry book.

Create an anthology of favourite verses

Illustrate your favourite verses.

Make up some rhymes to read or say to a group of younger children.

## Rhyming consequences

This is a game for children experienced with rhyme. They should have played rhyming games such as the above before trying this game. The aim of the game is to produce some fun four-line verses. It is another game that challenges verbal intelligence.

*Players*:       Any number, playing individually, in pairs or small teams

*Age range*:     Seven to adult

*Materials*:     Pen/pencil and paper

*How to play*

1   Each player writes the opening line of a poem on a blank piece of paper, and folds the paper over so that no-one can see what was written. The final word of the line is written again at the bottom of the page so that it can be seen by the next player.

2   The folded papers are passed on, and a new line is added by the next player which must  rhyme with the word written on the paper. The paper is folded again and the rhyming word written at the bottom of the page.

3   This process is repeated until all four lines have been written. Here is an example:

> The singer began to sing a song,
> He shouldn't have done what he knew was wrong,
> A man in a funny hat gave a shout
> There's a lot of this about.

Players must remember to make their writing as clear as possible, and to make sure that they end their lines with a word that has a rhyme.

4   The poems are unfolded and read out.

5   When play begins again players might want to try a longer poem, or a variation on the game such as allowing players to see the previous line before composing their own.

*Questions to think about*

- Would you have written a better poem if you knew what the previous line was? Why?

- Can you make sense of your finished poem? Can you say what it is about?

- Which of the verses that have been written in the game do you think is best? Why?

- What are 'consequences'? Why is the game called 'Rhyming *consequences*'?

- Would it be a better game if you could see the line before? What would make it a better or more interesting game?

- Did you enjoy playing this game? Why, or why not?

- Does this game help you to learn or think anything?

*Extension activities*

Create a variation of this game, for example 'Couplet Consequences' where players are allowed to see the first line of each rhyming couplet before composing their rhyming line.

Find and collect favourite examples of Nonsense Verse for a shared reading or anthology.

Use a rhyming dictionary to help you create some rhymed verse on a current topic of study.

# 5 Question games

If we want children to be flexible and adventurous thinkers we should encourage them to ask questions. The trouble is that as children get older they tend to ask fewer questions. A thinking child is a questioning child, and a thinking classroom or home is a place which invites questions as well as answers. The following are some games to help develop enquiry skills through encouraging children to question and to seek answers to questions.

# How many questions?

This game invites players to create as many questions as they can about a given object or idea. It is a game which encourages fluency, flexibility and variety of ideas. The winning player or team is the one to generate the longest and most varied list of questions.

*Players*: Any number, playing as individuals, pairs or groups.

*Age range*: Seven to adult

*Materials*: Pen/pencil and paper, and objects to question (see examples below)

*How to play*

Decide whether players are to play individually, in pairs or teams, and which object(s) or theme you will use as a stimulus for questions.

1 Present an object such as an ornament, machine or piece of furniture, and invite the players to write down as many questions as they can about that object within a specified time limit, for example ten minutes.

2 At the end of the given time limit the question-writing must stop. Questions are counted to see who has thought of most questions.

3 The player(s) with the longest list of questions read their questions out. No two questions must be the same, and players may challenge any they think are repeated in different words. The winners are those who have achieved a given target, say ten questions, or who have listed the most questions. Other forms of scoring are possible, for example scoring one point for every question and two for any that no other player or team has asked.

The following are some kinds of questions that can be asked about any object:

- physical features  What is it? What is it called? What does it look like? What colour is it? What shape is it? What texture is it? What does it feel like? Does it smell? Does it make a noise? What is it made of? Is it made of natural or artificial materials? Is it complete? Has it been altered or repaired?

- construction  How was it made? Who made it? Was it made by hand or machine? Was it made out of one piece or many pieces?

- function

  What was it made for? How could it be used? Where was it used? Was it used be a man or a woman? Can it be recycled?

- age

  Is it new or old? How old is it? How long will it last?

- value

  Is it valuable? To whom is it valuable? What is it worth?

- origin

  Where does it come from? Where was it made? What shop sells it?

- design

  Is it well designed? How is it decorated? How could it be improved?

*Questions to think about*

- Which do you think was the most interesting question you asked? Which was the most interesting question in the whole game?

- Which question(s) would you like to have answered?

- Are there different kinds of question? What kinds of question are there?

- How many questions is it possible to make up about any one object? (The answer is a limitless number.) Why? (No-one would know when such a list had ended!)

- Did other people ask different questions from you? Did any player ask exactly the same questions as any other? Why is this?

- If you played this game several times do you think you would get better at asking questions?

- Is it better to ask good questions, or a lot of questions? What is a good question?

*Extension activities*

Brainstorm as many questions as possible about a particular topic of study.

Choose an abstract idea like Love, Freedom, Friendship, Fairness, or War and Peace to ask questions about.

Research into non-fiction books or newspapers. What questions can you find?

Set up a Question Box for questions to be placed in during the week, and at the end of the week share the questions out for groups of children to discuss and try to answer.

Create your own questions and answers game, for example 'What's the Answer?':

## What's the answer?

*How to play*

In this game players are given slips of paper on which to write any question they choose. These can be for example knowledge questions like *Why are leaves green?*, personal questions like *How do I make friends?* or metaphysical questions like *What is the meaning of life?* These questions are written down, collected and shuffled. Each player is given one of the question papers and must write the best answer they can to the question they have been given. Invite players to share and discuss the question and answers given.

## Twenty questions

An old game but a good one for encouraging critical thinking, classification and questioning skills. There are a number of possible variations, but the following is the most common version.

*Players*:     Any number, playing as individuals

*Age range*:     Five to adult

*Materials*:     Pen/pencil and paper

*How to play*

Players try to discover the identity of the object within a limit of twenty questions.

1   Player 1 thinks of an object and declares it is either 'animal', 'vegetable' or 'mineral', or a combination of these.

2   Other players ask up to twenty questions to try to find out what this mystery object is. Their questions can only be answered by a 'yes' or 'no'.

3   Someone keeps a record of the number of questions asked. Player 1 wins if the mystery object remains undiscovered. Whoever guesses correctly can begin the next game.

To simplify the game the mystery object could be given a narrower category, for example a topic, an animal, a book title, form of transport, historical period, or geographic location.

*Questions to think about*
- What kind of game is this?
- Is this a game of luck or skill?
- Is everything in the world either 'animal', 'vegetable' or 'mineral' or a combination of these?
- How would you classify 'fear', 'hope' or 'love'?
- What is the best way (or strategy) to discover the mystery word in this game?
- What are the best kinds of questions?
- Can you (or did you) learn anything from this game?

*Extension activities*

Make classification taxonomies under the headings 'animal', 'vegetable' and 'mineral' ie what are the different categories that could come under these headings?

How would you classify the contents of the room you are in?

Ask groups to list members of a chosen set, for others to guess the classification title.

Create and play a variation on the Twenty Questions game, for example 'Who am I?':

# Who am I?

*How to play*

A player goes out of the room while the other players decide what well-known person, either real or fictional, the player will be. When this is decided the player is asked to return and has twenty questions to find out who he or she is. After the game discuss how you know who you are - do you know from what other people tell you or do you decide for yourself? Could you become someone else?

# Questions

The aim of this game is to keep a conversation going using only questions. It calls for quick thinking, verbal fluency and questioning skill.

*Players*:      Any number, playing in pairs

*Age range*:    Seven to adult

*Materials*:    None

## *How to play*

This is a speaking and listening game played in pairs. The challenge for the players is to keep a conversation going using only questions. Players must not repeat themselves or pause, and the  questions they ask must make sense, or they lose points. If a player loses three points the other player wins.

1   The first player asks a question, and the second player must reply with another question.

2   The two players must keep the conversation going as long as they can asking only questions. If a player pauses too long, repeats a question or asks a question which does not make sense they lose a point.

3   A player wins when the other player loses three points.

The following example of this game comes from the play *Rosencrantz and Guildenstern are Dead* by Tom Stoppard:

| | |
|---|---|
| GUILDENSTERN: | What's your name? |
| ROSENCRANTZ: | What's yours? |
| GUIL: | I asked first. |
| ROS: | Statement. One-love. |
| GUIL: | What's your name when you're at home? |
| ROS: | What's yours? |
| GUIL: | When I'm at home? |
| ROS: | Is it different at home? |
| GUIL: | What home? |
| ROS: | Haven't you got one? |
| GUIL: | Why do you ask? |
| ROS: | What are you driving at? |

GUIL:              *(With emphasis)* What's your name?

ROS:               Repetition. Two love.

*Questions to think about*

- Questions are one kind of sentence. What are other kinds of sentences called?

- Is it possible to hold a conversation by only asking questions?

- Did you find it difficult? What makes it difficult?

- Do you usually ask many questions? What kinds of questions do you ask?

- Is it good to ask questions? Why?

- Are there some people you would never ask a question? If so, why?

- Why do you think some people are afraid of asking questions? Can you give an example?

- Can you think of a question that does not have an answer?

*Extension activities*

Write a conversation or poem consisting only of questions.

Make a collage of questions cut out from newspapers, comics and magazines.

Compile a  list of questions with which to interview a local or famous personality.

Create a questionnaire to test people's views on a chosen subject like school or your neighbourhood.

Invent your own question and answer game, for example 'Questions and answers':

## Questions and answers

*How to play*

Players write down one answer to a question on a slip of paper. The papers are collected, shuffled and one given to each player who must think of and write down what as many questions as they can for which the answer could be given. The player with the most questions relevant to the given answer wins. Share and discuss the questions and answers.

# 6 Speaking and listening games

There is a close connection between talking and thinking. The following speaking games encourage participants to think before they speak, to engage in attentive listening, and to develop their verbal intelligence through discussion.

## Mystery voices

This is a game of deception in which players try to disguise their voices so that they cannot be recognised. The game encourages players to experiment with the sound of their voice and with voice projection and calls for attentive listening.

*Players*:      A large number of players, preferably more than ten

*Age range*:   Seven to adult

*Materials*:    None

*How to play*

Players take turns to try to identify the disguised voices of other players whom they cannot see. If they can identify the person from the voice they win, if not the player disguising their voice wins. The game can be played on an individual basis or as a team game.

1   The first player faces a wall, with eyes closed, and must not look round.

2   Three other players are chosen to be the 'mystery voices'. They stand behind but well back from the first player, and on a signal greets the first player in a disguised voice, saying for example : 'Hello Peter, how are you?'

3   The first player must guess which of the other players the mystery voice is. If in doubt they can ask for the mystery voice to repeat their sentence once more. The player is allowed only one guess.

4   If the guess is right the mystery voice says so, and the next mystery voice has a turn, saying the same sentence as the first eg 'Hello Peter, how are you?' If the first player guesses right the third mystery voice has a turn, and so on. If the first player guesses right they must not turn round. If the first player turns round they lose. If the first player guesses wrong they lose and can turn round to see who the mystery voice is. That person has the next turn to guess the mystery voice.

**5** Each player is given a turn, if they wish to be a mystery voice. Players wanting to be a mystery voice are chosen at random by the leader of the game. They should be encouraged to use as strange a voice as they can. Players may be allowed a few minutes before the game to practise their mystery voices, The winner is the player who recognises most mystery voices.

*Questions to think about*

- Is everybody's voice different? Give reasons why this might be so.

- Can everybody disguise their own voice? Are some better at it than others? Give examples.

- Do you find it easy to disguise your voice?

- Do you find it easy to recognise everyone even if they disguise their voices?

- Which people need to disguise their voices in real life?

- What is your favourite way of disguising your voice? Why is it your favourite voice disguise?

- Do you like your voice? Would you like to change the sound of your voice? Why? Could you do it? How?

- Are people's voices part of who they are? Does that mean that if they change their voice they are changing themselves? Are they then the same person?

- What would life be like without a voice?

- What would life be like if every voice sounded the same?

*Extension activities*

Tape record some disguised voices to try to identify, or the voices of people known to the players.

Challenge players to read a passage or poem in a given accent.

Play other voice games such as 'Chinese Whispers':

# Chinese whispers

*How to play*

The object of the game is to see how a sentence or short story changes as it passes round a group of speakers. Players sit in a circle and the first player thinks of a message and whispers it to the next player. The second player whispers it to the third player and so on round the circle until it returns to the first player. The player says what the message has become, and how it started. Often the two versions are very different.

# Just a minute

Players are asked to speak on a chosen subject for a given length of time, such as a minute.

*Players:*      Any number, playing individually

*Age range:*   Seven to adult

*Materials:*    A list of topics, seconds timer, pen/pencil and paper (optional)

*How to play*

Ask individuals to speak to the rest of the group for just a minute without hesitation, repetition or deviation from the given subject. This works better if players are given some 'thinking time' in which to prepare what they are going to say. They may make notes, but should not use these when giving their talk.

The simplest version of the game is as follows:

1   An individual tries to talk for one minute on a given topic.

2   The talk is timed by a referee.

3   The speaker wins if the talk lasts one minute.

A harder version is for the speaker to talk for a minute without hesitation, repetition (of nouns, verbs or adjectives), or deviation from the subject.

A simpler version is to have a target of half a minute.

*Questions to think about*

*   Is it easier to talk about something you have had time to think about beforehand?

- Would it be easier to remember what to say if you wrote it down first?

- Is it hard to talk in front of a large group of people? If it is hard, what makes it hard?

- What helps you to talk in front of a large group of people?

- Does this game help you to be a better speaker in front of people?

- What would help you be a better speaker and talker?

- What is the difference between speaking and giving a talk or speech?

- Is it better to talk a little or a lot? Explain why. Give an example.

- What do you think, and feel, when giving a talk or speech?

*Extension activities*

Ask players to prepare a speech on a chosen subject to last longer than a minute eg five minutes.

Find out from the *Guinness Book of Records* who has made the longest speech.

Listen carefully when someone gives a talk. How much of it can you remember?

Take notes when someone gives a talk. Does it help you recall what was said?

Tape record yourself playing this game, or giving a talk to others.

Write what you think a good talk or speech is. What in giving a talk are you good at? What are you not good at? What would help you be a better speaker?

Play your own variation on Just a Minute, for example 'Telephone!':

# Telephone!

*How to play*

For this game you need one or two telephones (unconnected). Players take turns to speak on the telephone to an imaginary person who has telephoned them. After speaking for one minute, they can hand the telephone to the next player saying there is a call for them. Players gain a point if they can sustain an imaginary conversation for one minute without undue hesitation or repetition. Discuss afterwards how talking on the telephone differs from talking face to face.

# The minister's cat

A traditional speaking game that can be adapted to different themes and purposes. It is a useful 'warm-up' activity to encourage quick thinking and a useful prelude to further thinking or discussion activities. It is principally about the use of adjectives, but also challenges alphabetic knowledge.

*Players*:      Any number playing as a group

*Age range*:   Seven to adult

*Materials*:    None needed

*How to play*

The game is best played with everyone sitting or standing in a circle. It is a 'follow-on' game. If a player cannot follow on when their turn comes they are out of the game.

1  The first person says the following words: 'The minister's cat is an cat, and his/her name is ...' An adjective beginning with 'A' is said before the word 'cat' and the name is given, also beginning with 'A'.

2  The next person has to repeat the words, this time adding an adjective and a name beginning with 'B'. This pattern is repeated through the alphabet and when 'Z' is reached the game starts again. The aim is to follow the last person as quickly as possible. If there is too long a gap, say over ten seconds, that player is out. No adjective or person's name can be repeated during the game. No name of any other player can be used. When 'X' comes a player is allowed to use 'ex' eg as in 'expert' or 'exceptional'.

3  The player(s) left playing at the end of the game or at the end of a given time win.

The following is part of a game in practice: 'The minister's cat is ...

> an angry cat and his name is Arthur
> a bald cat and his name is Balthazar
> a creepy cat and her name is Camilla
> a dribbling cat and his name is Denis
> an eerie cat and his name is Eric
> a fat cat and her name is Fergie
> a gorgeous cat and his name is George ...'

*Questions to think about*

- Are you better at quick thinking, as in this game, or slow thinking? Can you give a reason?
- Do you think you learn anything from this game? What do you learn?
- Would it help to play using a dictionary? Why?

*Extension activities*

Play the game as a writing activity.

Play the game allowing the use of dictionaries.

Play the game in a foreign language (if the players know or are learning another language).

Devise your own version of the game.

Play other alphabet games such as saying the alphabet backwards, or 'Alphabet travelling':

## Alphabet travelling

*How to play*

Each player asks the player on their left two questions: 'Where are you going?' and 'What will you do there?' The replies must contain a place (town or country) and description of an activity (with verb, adjective and noun), for example 'Barnsley' and 'Buying beautiful bicycles'. The first player replies with answers beginning with 'A', the second player with 'B' and so on through the alphabet. Each word in the answer must begin with the same letter. Allow 20 seconds to reply.

## Random words

This game involves making, and avoiding, conceptual connections between random words. It is a useful 'warm-up' activity to encourage quick thinking, and can lead to discussion about connections and the meanings of words.

*Players*:      Any number, playing individually or in teams

*Age range*:   Seven to adult

*Materials*:    None

*How to play*

Players take turns in saying random words, while other players try to find a connection between any two consecutive words. If they can find a connection they get a point. It helps if players sit or stand in a circle.

1   A player starts by saying any word. Other players in turn say a new word which has no connection whatever with the previous word. Players can challenge if they think they can see a connection between a word and the previous word. They can only challenge before the next person speaks, otherwise the game continues.

2   A player who spots a connection must signal before the next word is spoken, and say what the connection is between the last two spoken words. A player drops out if there is hesitation, repetition or a connection is spotted. The following is an example of play with each player saying a word: 'Pig, kettle, vest, flower, piano, sunshine, spoon, fork … 'Challenge!', shouted a player, 'spoon and fork are both cutlery.'

3   The player spotting a connection earns a point (alternatively the person saying the connected word, 'fork' in the example above, is out). Discussion may ensue about whether a real connection has been made. Differences of opinion can be resolved by the decision of an impartial umpire, or by majority vote.

*Questions to think about*
- Is everything like something else?
- Is there anything that is not like something else?
- This game is called 'random words'. What does random mean? Can you give examples?
- What things in the world are random?
- Does this game help your thinking or learning?
- Did you enjoy this game? Why, or why not?
- What would make this a better game?

*Extension activities*

Play the game with a partner. Record the game. Analyse it afterwards. Did you miss any connections?

Play other connection games, such as those on p 12.

Invent your own connection game.

## Balloon debates

A balloon debate is a problem solving task in which a group is asked to decide who is the most important member of a given list, or who is the least important. Usually the debate is stimulated by a story in which either one person must be thrown from a leaking balloon to keep it airborne, or all must be thrown leaving only the most deserving survivor. The debate in either case is over who should be the chosen one.

*Players*:      Any number, playing individually, in pairs or in small groups

*Age range*:    Nine to adult

*Materials*:    Pen/pencil and paper

*How to play*

Present a balloon debate scenario, for example:

Up to ten famous people are crowded in a basket suspended beneath a hot air balloon. Unfortunately the balloon has a slow leak. The only way to keep the balloon airborne and prevent it from crashing and killing everyone is to throw someone out. The problem is to decide which person in the basket is most worth preserving.

1  List the ten people in the balloon. (These can be chosen by you, or suggested by the players before the game starts).

2  Ask each player, pair or group to decide which of the ten they think is most worth preserving for the future of humankind. The players should note down all the possible reasons for their choices, including defence against any possible reasons for not choosing their candidate. Players or groups should decide how best to put their argument, and which part of the case each player will put across. Allow 10-15 minutes for this.

3  Have the groups come forward for the debate in a formal arrangement. each speaker/group should present their case to the audience as a whole.

**4** Having heard each case and all the arguments the audience votes on which candidate they think has the most convincing case for survival. The announcement of the survivor ends the activity.

*Questions to think about*

- What is a debate? How does it differ from a conversation, discussion or argument?
- What did you learn from taking part in the balloon debate?
- Was it a fair debate?
- Where do other debates take place?
- What rules should there be in a debate?
- Is voting a fair way to decide a debate ? Why?
- What would be other good topics for a debate?
- Would it ever be right to kill person? If so, when and why? If not, why not?

*Extension activities*

Hold a debate on another topic. The following are some alternative topics for debate:

- *The best form of transport* for the general public is: car, bicycle, bus, train, roller-blades, horse?
- *The most useful subject* for study in school is: English. maths, science, technology, history, geography, PE, art, music or RE?
- *The best spare-time activity* is: reading, watching TV, playing on the computer, cooking, swimming, playing football, shopping?

Hold a debate on a topic chosen by the children

Research arguments from a recent debate in the media eg TV, newspapers.

# 7 Story games

Story games are as old as Homer. In modern times the oral tradition is largely confined to jokes, anecdotes and gossip. The following games provide opportunities to exercise verbal intelligence and story-telling skills.

## Story chain

Story chain games provide opportunities for developing language skills in sequencing and building on ideas to create and complete a group story. Players must think quickly in order to continue a given train of narrative thought

*Players*:       Any number, playing as a group

*Age range*:   Five to adult

*Materials*:    None

*How to play*

With the group sitting in a circle the leader begins a story, and each member must continue the story in turn. If players are allowed to stop their part of the story when they like it means that even the shyest can make a short contribution. The following is a simple form of the game.

1   Players sit in a circle. One player is chosen as leader and begins a story.

2   At any point the story teller can stop, even in mid-sentence, and the next player must continue the story where it left off.

3   This player stops at any time, and the next player continues the story and so on.

4   Players who pause too long, or who cannot continue, miss their turn or are out of the game.

The following are some variations on this game:

- each player adds only one sentence

- each player must finish in mid-sentence

- the story-teller throws an object eg a ball to anyone in the circle who must continue the story.

*Questions to think about*

- Did you find continuing the story easy or difficult? Why?

- Was it a good story that your group made up in the game? What was good, or not good, about it?

- Do you prefer to make up stories with other people or by yourself? Why?

- Do you know of any other stories made up by more than one person? Can you give examples?

- What is a story? Can you give a definition of what a story is?

- Could you make up a never-ending story? Can you give an example of a never-ending story?

- What is your favourite story? Why?

- What different kinds of story are there? What is your favourite kind of story?

- Who is your favourite story-teller? Why?

- What is the earliest story you can remember hearing?

*Extension activities*

Try to remember and summarise the story chain in all its detail.

Write your own version of the story told in the game.

Record a story chain for others to listen to.

Play a variation of the story chain game, for example 'Story Battle' or 'Chainwriting':

## Story battle

*How to play*

Two teams of players face each other. The first player in Team A starts the story, stopping at any point. The first player of Team B then tries to subvert the story with a continuation that begins 'but ...' stopping at any point. The second player of Team A then tries to re-establish the story along the original lines, the next player of Team B tries to subvert or end the story, the next from Team A to revive the story and so on.

## Chainwriting

*How to play*

Each player adds to a written story, seeing only the previous sentence.
The first player begins writing a sentence across the top of a sheet of
paper. The second reads this and continues writing the story, then
folds it over so only the previous sentence can be read and passes it to
the next player and so on. When all players have contributed a
sentence the first player reads the whole story to the group.

## Picture story

Every picture tells a story but can the players make a story from every
picture? Can they translate the visual into the creatively verbal? This
game challenges them to do just that.

*Players*:        Any number, playing individually, in pairs or in small
                  groups

*Age range*:      Seven to adult

*Materials*:      A set of pictures, reproductions of works of art.

*How to play*

Collect a set of large pictures or reproductions of works of art (such as
the *Active Art Picture Pack* ed. R. Fisher, published by Stanley Thornes)
which have potential narrative interest.

1   The first player (pair or team of players) is given a picture to look
    at.

2   The player is then asked to make up a story about the picture. The
    story must refer to some of the visual elements in the picture.

3   If the game is played in pairs or teams any member may take up the
    story at any point.

*Questions to think about*

• Does every picture tell a story?

• Can you tell a story about every picture?

• How many different stories do you think could be told about your
  picture?

• Does it help to have someone else telling the story with you?

- What makes a good story?
- What makes for a good picture to make up a story from?
- Which is your favourite picture? Why?
- Which was your favourite story? Why?

*Extension activities*

Players are given two pictures and must create a story which links both pictures. Then three or more pictures may be used as episodes in the same story.

Write a  story or poem about your picture. Make a copy of the picture to go with the story.

Draw or paint a picture from which others must construct a story.

From a  given picture players must create a mime, or play, about what happened before, during and after the scene of the picture.

# Alphabet stories

A challenging game in which every word of a story must begin with the same letter of the alphabet. The game involves using creativity and imagination and calls for verbal fluency.

*Players*:  Any number, playing individually, in pairs or small groups.

*Age range*:  Nine to adult

*Materials*:  Pen/pencil and paper, dictionaries (optional)

*How to play*

Players choose a letter of the alphabet, for example 'A' and try to write a story in which every word begins with 'A'. Younger players may be allowed the use of dictionaries. After a given period of time, say 15 minutes, the stories are read out. Players discuss which story they think is the best.

*Questions to think about*

- Was it hard to write an alphabet story? What were the reasons for this?
- How many different words did you use?

- How many different words in the dictionary are there beginning with your chosen letter?

- Is the best story necessarily the longest story? Why?

- What is a story? Is every piece of writing a story? What does writing have to have to become a story?

- What makes a good story?

- Which of the alphabet stories that were written in your game was the best? Why do you think so?

*Extension activities*

Create an alphabet story book, with the best stories containing words beginning with only one letter of the alphabet.

Illustrate your alphabet story.

Play other alphabet story games, for example where each player or team must try to make up a story using each successive letter of the alphabet from A-Z.

Play other story writing games, for example where each player or team must write an interesting mini-saga or short story in only 50 words.

# 8 Word games

Word games such as Scrabble create opportunities for strategic thinking and the development of verbal intelligence. Word games can be played mechanically and without much evidence of thinking, but they can also provide puzzles of logical and linguistic challenge, and can stimulate children to develop their own creative wordplay. Play with words invigorates our use of language and our thinking about language. Again the move needs to be made between spontaneous practice and considered reflection through discussion. The following activities encourage players to explore and extend their vocabulary and knowledge about language. Word games can encourage a lively interest in words, and help develop an ability to use words more confidently and thoughtfully.

The following are examples of word games worth thinking about:

## Square words

Crosswords is one of the best of all word games. It is deceptively simple, and can be played in many different variations. It was a popular Victorian pastime, and was a favourite game of the Reverend Dodgson (Lewis Carroll). Scrabble and other popular word games have been developed from this simple yet sophisticated game.

Square words is a competitive form of word squares or crosswords. It has great potential for developing language awareness and thinking skills, if it is used as a Thinking Game.

*Players*:     Any number, playing in pairs, in small or as one large groups

*Age range*:     Seven to adult

*Materials*:     Pen/pencil and paper

*How to play*

<u>Game 1</u>

The object of the game is to make words across and down a crossword grid of 25 squares.

1   Each player draws a grid of 5 x 5 squares.

2   The first player calls out a letter. Each player writes that letter in any square on their grid, and keeps their grid hidden from other players.

3   The next player then chooses a letter which each player enters on any space in their grid to help them make a word. This continues with each player in turn choosing a letter for all players to enter on a vacant square of their grid.

4   Letters are chosen in turn until all the squares of the grid have been filled ie 25 letters. No changing or rubbing out of letters is allowed!

It is a good idea to write a list for all to see of the letters as they are chosen so that players can check which letters they should have used during and at the end of the game. Letters may be repeated any number of times. Thinking time should be allowed between each letter.

**5** At the end of play the grids are exchanged for marking.

A good scoring system is as follows:

10 points for a five letter word
5 points for a four letter word
3 points for a three letter word
2 points for a two letter word

The usual word game rules apply. Only words that can be found in a dictionary are allowed ie no proper nouns etc. No letter may form part of two words on a line.

The following is an example of how a grid might look at the finish of a game.

| S | D | R | I | P |
|---|---|---|---|---|
| T | A | M | E | C |
| E | O | U | J | W |
| E | N | D | O | A |
| P | L | A | Y | H |

The total number of points scored in this game was: drip (5), tame (5), end (3), play (5), steep (10), on (2), mud (3), joy (3), ah (2) = 38

*Questions to think about*

- Which letter of the alphabet appears in the greatest number of English words?

- What letters are the easiest to make words with? Which are the hardest?

- Does it help to have thinking time? How much time should there be between each turn?

- Are there any strategies for placing the letters that help you make more words?

- What was the ratio of vowels to consonants in your game? Would it have helped to have more vowels or consonants?

- Did you enjoy this game? Why, or why not?

- In what ways does a game like this help you think or learn?

*Extension activities*

Create your own variation on the Crossword game, for example playing on a 6 x 6 grid.

Call all the 25 letters in the game then see who can make the highest score with them, using trial and improve methods.

Play the crossword game in a foreign language that you know or are learning.

Create your own symmetrical crossword design by colouring in blank squares on a grid.

Design your own traditional crossword puzzle, with a clue invented for each word.

## Jotto

Jotto is an old game that encourages logical thinking, and is the forerunner of modern games of logic like Mastermind.

*Players*:      Any number, playing in pairs

*Age range*:    Seven to adult

*Materials*:    Pen/pencil and paper, dictionaries optional.

*How to play*

The aim is to discover your opponent's secret word.

1  Each player writes down a secret word of four, five or six letters, and says how many letters their secret word contains.

2  The first player calls out a word of similar length to the other player's secret word.

3  The second player must then say how many letters it has in common with his secret word. For example if the secret word is

'SCHOOL' , and the player guesses 'STABLE', the first player would say 'two letters'.

4 The first to correctly identify the other player's secret word is the winner.

Note: To make the game easier players could say the names of the letters as well as how many are common in the two words.

*Questions to think about*
- Did you find this an easy or hard game to play? Why?
- What kinds of words would be hardest to discover?
- What letters are the most common in words?
- What letters are the least common?
- Is this a game of luck or skill?
- Are there any strategies that might help you to discover the secret word?
- Could you learn anything from this game?

*Extension activities*

Investigate the game of Mastermind. How is Jotto similar and different to Mastermind?

Try playing this game using longer words, or different rules.

Investigate other 'secret word' games, such as codes. Invent your own code and coded message.

Play related word games such as Letterlogic, p 85.

# Word maze

Word maze is a game where children are asked to find as many letter routes through a word square as they can in a given time.

*Players*:    Any number
*Age range*:    Seven to adult
*Materials*:    Pen/pencil and paper or photocopied word squares, coloured pens/pencils

*How to play*

Children are shown or given a word square such as the following:

| P | R | O | B |
|---|---|---|---|
| R | O | B | L |
| O | B | L | E |
| B | L | E | M |

1 Children are given the challenge of seeing how many letter routes to make the word PROBLEM they can find through this word maze. They can trace different routes with different coloured pens/pencils.

2 The winners are those who have identified the maximum number of routes within a given time.

3 Players may try to create their own word mazes for future rounds.

*Questions to think about*

• What is a maze?

• Is there a maze in this game? Why, or why not?

• What is the maximum number of letter routes through this maze?

• Is there a strategy for finding all the possible letter routes?

• Can you apply this strategy to any other problems?

• What did you think or learn during this game?

• What kind of game is this?

*Extension activities*

Can you create a word maze using another word?

Can you create a word maze of a different shape?

Investigate the word mazes that you or other people in your group create.

## Acrossword

A simple crossword game which encourages thinking about words.

*Players*:    Any number, playing as individuals or in pairs

*Age range*:   Seven to adult

*Materials*:   Pen/pencil and paper, dictionaries (optional)

*How to play*

The aim of the game is to create the longest words possible between a given set of first and last letters. The game can be played with or without the help of dictionaries.

1   Choose a long word. Players must write this word down the left-hand side of the paper, and then write the same word backwards down the right-hand side of their paper.

2   Players must now find words that will fit between each pair of letters. For example if the word DEMOCRACY is chosen, this is how it would be written at the start of the game:

| D | | Y |
|---|---|---|
| E | | C |
| M | | A |
| O | | R |
| C | | C |
| R | | O |
| A | | M |
| C | | E |
| Y | | D |

Here is how one player fitted in his words during a game:

| D | | E | L | | A | | Y |
|---|---|---|---|---|---|---|---|
| E | | | P | | | I | C |
| M | A | L | A | | R | I | A |
| O | | F | | F | | E | R |
| C | | O | | M | | I | C |
| R | | A | | D | | I | O |
| A | | L | B | | U | | M |
| C | | R | | A | | N | E |
| Y | | | A | | R | | D |

**3** One point is scored for each letter. The player or team with the highest score wins (In the above game the player scored 45 points. Can you do better?)

*Questions to think about*

- Were you good at this game? Why do you think that was?

- What is your longest word? What does the long word you have chosen mean? What is its origin?

- Where do the meanings of words come from? Who decides what words mean?

- Could a word mean anything you wanted it to mean? Why?

- Are the longest words the hardest to spell? Why? Can you give examples?

- Which letter of the alphabet begins more words in English than any other? Which letter ends more words than any other? How could you find out?

- What did you think or learn from this game?

*Extension activities*

Have a *backwards* spelling quiz ie spelling words backwards.

Try playing this game with words from foreign languages. What is the longest word in a foreign language you can find?

Which long word will allow you, your group or class to create the highest Acrossword score?

# The list game

A vocabulary game that involves players brainstorming words to match a number of given categories. The game can be played in a number of variations.

*Players*:       Any number, playing individually or in pairs

*Age range*:   Seven to adult

*Materials*:    Pen/pencil and paper

*How to play*

Each player has a pencil and paper. A list of categories is written down the left hand side of the page. Any categories will do, for example a selection of the following – animal, vegetable, mineral, fruit, fish, flower, bird, insect, country, town, street name, river, author, book, title, boys' names, girls' names, games, TV programme etc.

1 Having listed the categories choose a letter, and allow everyone five or ten minutes to write down as many names as they can against each category. Each name must begin with the chosen letter.

2 At the end of the game each player scores two points for each word in their list that no-one has thought of, and one mark for words which others have thought of.

3 A new letter is then chosen and the game begins afresh.

Note: One way to choose a random letter is to identify a letter in a book, for example: 'Find the third letter in the fifth word on the tenth line on page 79.'

*Questions to think about*
• The list game is about putting words in categories. What is a category?

• Which category has the most names? Why is this?

• Do some names belong to more than one category? Can you give examples?

• Are there some things that do not fit into any category? If so, give an example. If not, why not?

• Does everything in the world have a  name? Where do these names come from?

• This is a list game. Do you make lists in your life? When, and why?

• What famous lists are there? Can you remember any lists?

*Extension activities*
Create your own list game.

Create your own book of lists, using reference books like the *Guinness Book of Records* to help you.

Play other list games in this book.

# Place names

This is a list game using geographical place names, each of which must begin with a chosen letter.

*Players*:      Any number, playing individually or in pairs

*Age range*:    Seven to adult

*Materials*:    Pen/pencil and paper; atlas, globe or maps (optional)

*How to play*

1   A letter is chosen at random. All players write down every geographical place name they can think of beginning with that letter. Younger children may be given an atlas, globe or map to help them.

2   After a set time the game stops. One player reads out their list. Everyone totals their score, gaining two points for a name which no-one has thought of, and one mark for a name that one or more other players have on their list.

3   A new letter is chosen and the game restarts.

*Questions to think about*

• Does every place have a name? Do some places have more than one name? Why? Give examples.

• What is a 'place'?

• Where do the names of places come from?

• Do you know the names of any imaginary places? Describe one of these places.

• What is the name of your favourite place? Describe this place.

• What is your least favourite place? Describe it, and say why you do not like it.

• Where could you look to find out information about different places?

*Extension activities*

Research the origin of place names.

Play a variation on the Place Name game, for example write GEOGRAPHY down the side of the page, and ask players to write as many place names as they can against each letter.

Devise your own version of the Place Name game.

Debate where you would most like to live, or to have a holiday.

Invent your own imaginary place. Compile a guidebook about it.

Draw, paint or model your own imaginary Shangri-La.

## The name game

This list game is based on people's names.

*Players*:      Any number, playing individually or in pairs

*Age range*:   Seven to adult

*Materials*:    Pen/pencil and paper

*How to play*

1   One of the players chooses a name, for example ROBERT, which all write down the left hand side of their page, one letter under another.

2   Players must write down as many first names as they can think of beginning with each key letter. Allow five minutes.

3   The winner is the one to write most names.

*Questions to think about*

- Does everyone have a name?  Why, or why not?

- Who chose your name? Why was that name chosen?

- If you had a different name what name or names would you choose? Why choose that name?

- If you had a different name would you be a different person?

- Is your name important to you? Would it matter if people called you by any name they chose? Why?

- Why are names so important to people?

- Are you good at remembering names? What can help you to remember names?

*Extension activities*

Research the origins of names.

Write an acrostic poem based on your own, or someone else's name.

Invent a calligraphic design based on your own or someone else's name.

Create as many words as you can out of the letters in your name

# Word hunt

Word hunt involves taking a long word and finding out how many shorter words can be made using its letters. The game can be played on a co-operative or competitive basis. The co-operative version involves the whole group hunting for the maximum number of words they can find. The competitive version involves seeing how many words individual players can find using the letters of a given word.

*Players*:   Any number, playing individually

*Age range*:   Seven to adult

*Materials*:   Pen/pencil and paper, dictionary (optional)

*How to play*

A long word, such as CHRYSANTHEMUM or EXPLORATION, is chosen as the target for the word hunt. The game is more difficult if words are chosen which have a limited number of vowels. For an easier version choose a key phrase, such as MERRY CHRISTMAS or HAPPY BIRTHDAY.

1   Players are asked how many words they can make from a given word, for example from RHINOCEROS would come ON, NOSE, ROSE, CHIN, HORN, SORE, SHINE etc.

2   Players list the words they can find within a set time. No proper names or abbreviations are allowed, only words that could be found in a dictionary.

3   At the end of the game lists are checked. Whoever has found the most words wins. A good way to score is to give players 1 point for every word and 2 points for any word no other player has found. Another way to score is by letter, that is 2 points for a 2 letter word, 3 points for a 3 letter word and so on.

*Questions to think about*

• What is a word?

• How were words created? Where do they come from?

• Is there a maximum number of words that could be made from the letters of any one word?

- How could you check you had found all the possible words?

- How did you hunt for words? Did you have a strategy for trying to make up words from the letters? Why did you use that strategy?

- Do you prefer to play by yourself or with a partner? Why?

- Is there a strategy for hunting words in a systematic way?

- Is this a useful game to play? Why? What did you learn from playing this game?

- What would be a good target word for the word hunt game?

- What is the longest word you know, or can find?

*Extension activities*

Play 'Target word hunt' which involves writing a nine letter word in a square and players trying to make as many words as they can including the middle or target letter. For example the word DISLOCATE provides the target letter O and gives words such as COT, COAT, TOE, SOLID, ISOLATE etc.:

D   I   S

L   O   C

A   T   E

Collect and play word hunt games like Lexicon, Scrabble etc.

Invent your own word hunt game.

## Scrambled words (or anagrams)

A scrambled word is a word whose letters have been jumbled up, such as 'hosloc' for 'school'. An anagram is a special kind of scrambled word formed by using the letters of a word or phrase and changing the order to make another word which makes sense. For example 'meat' is an anagram for 'team', 'hire tent' is an anagram for 'thirteen'. The challenge in this game is to rearrange a set of letters, or an anagram, to form a new word.

*Players*:      Any number, playing individually or in pairs

*Age range*:   Seven to adult

*Materials*:    Pen/pencil and paper

## How to play

Prepare a number of scrambled words (or anagrams) ready for the game, or ask half the players to devise anagrams or scrambled words for the others to solve. These words can be random, or related to a theme, such as scrambled cities eg nodonl, sirap, more, wen roky, loos, scomwo, lucatact, tonginwash, kooty, lerbin etc. The following are examples of anagrams: shore (horse), acre (care/race), lump (plum), bleat (table), arts (rats/atar), asleep (please), cheap (peach), earth (heart), words (sword), disease (seaside).

1  Each player or pair of players is given a number of scrambled words (anagrams) to solve in a given time. They should be told not to spend too long on any one puzzling word, but go on to the next.

2  When the time is up the game stops.

3  The players who have solved most or all of the anagrams win.

## Questions to think about

• What can you learn from this kind of word game?

• Do you have a strategy for trying to find the hidden word? What do you do?

• Do you find this an easy or difficult game? Why?

• Do you prefer to work out the words by yourself, or with a partner? Why?

• Do you prefer to try to work out scrambled words, or to make up your own scrambled words? Why?

• Does a dictionary help? Why?

• What is your opinion of this game? What are its good and bad points?

## Extension activities

Create your own scrambled words using categories such as countries, birds, flowers or animals – or words from an current topic of study.

Play a variation on scrambled words, for example create some scrambled words or anagrams for players to find in a sentence as in the following:

| A teacher's job is to cheat | (cheat = teach) |
| Police have to crate missing persons | (crate = trace) |
| He had to walk over a lime to get home | (lime = mile) |
| The tiles on the roof were made of steal | (steal = slate) |

Play other scrambled letter games, such as:

## Dice words

*How to play*

Stick letters on the faces of six die. Roll the die and see how many words players can make from the six letters on view. One point for each letter in a different word they can make. For example what word score can you make from these letters – S, R, M, A, E, T?

Invent your own scrambled word game.

## Scrambled sentences

This game will encourage young players to feel that they have some control over the creation of sentences. It will help develop editing skills, and the creative thinking that will help them to rearrange and extend their writing.

*Players*:       Any number, playing individually, in pairs or teams

*Age range*:   Five to adult

*Materials*:     Pen/pencil and paper or card

*How to play*

In preparation for the game sentences will need to be written on a piece of paper or card and cut up into single words (be careful not to mix words from different sentences!). One way is for each player write and cut up their own sentences without showing the rest of the group. Begin with simple sentences, and move on to more complex sentences as the game and players' skill develops.

1    Each player, pair or team is given a set of single words written on pieces of paper or card that can be reconstructed into a sentence.

2    On a given signal players begin to try reconstructing the given words into a sentence.

3    The first player, pair or team succeeding to make a grammatical and meaningful sentence wins, or whichever players succeed in a given time win.

*Questions to think about*

- What is a sentence? What is the shortest sentence you know or can find?

- Can a sentence be any length? What is the longest sentence you can find in a book or newspaper? (Can you find a sentence longer than the first sentence of Dickens' *A Tale of Two Cities*?)

- How many different sentences can be made out of the words of the English language? (Answer: an infinity, or at least more than can ever be counted).

- .Can every sentence be rewritten in other words, and keep the same meaning?

- If a sentence is rewritten in other words will it have the same meaning? Can you give an example?

- Can there be a meaningless sentence? Can you give an example?

- What do you think are the most important sentences ever written or spoken?

*Extension activities*

Invent or play a variation of this game, for example:

## Scrambled paragraphs

*How to play*

Choose an article from a newspaper, journal, encyclopaedia or reference book and cut out or reproduce paragraphs for the players to try to reconstruct the article. Compare and discuss the results with the original reference article.

## Divided sentences

*How to play*

Each group writes a meaningful sentence of about 25 words, then divides it into three sentences (adding any necessary words). Swap the sentences between groups and see which group can reconstruct the original sentence (omitting words if necessary).

## Sentence building games

*How to play*

Each member of a team writes down a word. These are then put together and shown to the group, who try to make sentences out of them by adding extra words. Groups who make most sentences with their words win. For the next round each player chooses two words, or three. Can players make up sentences without adding any extra words?

Other sentence-building games involve players being given four letters, such as AENH, or the initial letters of a word such as 'summer', with which to make as many sentences as they can in a given time with words beginning with those letters, for example AENH could make 'African elephants need help'. The players making most (sensible) sentences win.

## Readaround

This reading game encourages prediction, using context clues and thinking about the meanings of words and sentences.

*Players*:      Any number, playing in groups

*Age range*:    Five to adult

*Materials*:    A book, or set of books, of suitable reading level for the players

*How to play*

1  Players sit in a circle or group, with one or more copies of a suitable reading book.

2  The player who is picked as the first reader begins reading from the book, without showing others the page that is being read.

3  The reader stops after the first word of a new sentence. The next player eg on the left must guess the next word. If the guess is wrong the reader reads the word, and the next player tries to guess the next word, and so on.

4  When a player guesses correctly they become the new reader. The reader finishes the sentence and passes the book to the new reader who chooses a new passage and so on as before.

5  If a sentence is finished without anyone guessing a word correctly the reader passes the book to the next player who becomes the next reader and so on.

Players sometimes prefer a version where everyone in the group may guess at each word.

*Questions to think about*

- Is it easy or difficult to guess the next word? Why?

- Which kinds of word are easy to guess and which are more difficult? Why is this?

- Is it easier to guess the word near the beginning or near the end of sentences? Why?

- How many different ways do you think there are of finishing any sentence?

- How many different words are there in the English language?

- What is a prediction?

- Do you predict what is going to happen in a story when you are reading a book? Why?

- Do you prefer to read a book, or have it read to you? Why? Does it depend on what book it is?

*Extension activities*

Play a variation on Readaround to encourage prediction, for example:

# Mystery lines

*How to play*

Players choose a mystery book from a given set, and each player reads the first and last lines from the book. Other players must guess the title of the book being read. Or a player reads an excerpt from a book which includes at least one character's name (but in the reading gives a grunt instead of reading the character's name). Can other players guess which book, which character(s) feature in the book, and who the author is?

# What happened next?

*How to play*

A player reads a passage which ends with a character about to do one of two (or more) things. The reading stops, and the reader gives the alternative courses of action (including the real outcome in the book). Other players must predict what happens next.

## Missing words

*How to play*

Prepare a reading by deleting ten adjectives or other chosen words from the passage. The passage is read and each missing word is indicated. The reader pauses while players write down what word they think is missing. Players may ask for the piece to be read again. Finally the piece is read with the missing words in place. Players who guessed the right word get two points, if they guessed a wrong word but one which made sense they get one point.

Write different ways of finishing a chosen sentence or passage in a book. Discuss which sentence or passage completed by players is most interesting, and consider which was nearest to the way the author finished the sentence or passage.

## Speedwriting

From the brain, through the arm, via the pen onto the paper. Speedwriting provides a challenging game that helps players realise how much they are capable of writing in a short space of time. Other names for this game are 'Speed marathon', and 'Composition derby'. The idea is that players experience the flow of writing without serious concern with content or spelling.

*Players*:      Any number, playing individually

*Age range*:    Seven to adult

*Materials*:    Pen/pencil and plenty of paper!

*How to play*

Players sit with only a pen or pencil and a plentiful supply of paper. The aim of the game is to see how much they can write in a given time. The essence is speed, and as this is a draft they need not worry about spelling or punctuation errors, but the writing must be legible enough for someone else to read. They can write whatever they want, but it must make sense, and must not repeat themselves. They  are allowed to write in a 'stream of consciousness', for example if they get stuck could write 'I can't think of anything to write at the moment' or 'I'm stuck at the moment, and thinking what to write. I think I'll write about what happened yesterday ...'

1   Players are given five minutes to write as much as they can as fast as they can. They begin when a signal is given.

**2** The timekeeper tells players when each minute goes by.

**3** After the time is up all writing stops.

**4** Players exchange their writing, read each other's work and count the number of words written.

**5** The player who has written the most or achieved a specified target length wins.

It is useful for players to record their performance, so that in future games they can compete against their previous best speedwriting effort.

*Questions to think about*

- Can you write as fast as you can think? Why is this?

- Are you good at the speedwriting game? Why do you think so?

- Could you get better at speedwriting? How might you get better at it?

- Is it useful to be able to write quickly like this? Why? When might it be useful?

- Are you able to write faster on some occasions and not others? If so, why? If not, why not?

- Did playing the speedwriting game tell you anything about yourself as a thinker or writer?

- Some people prefer to think slowly, and others like to think quickly. What kind of thinker are you?

- Would you like to change, and to think more slowly or more quickly? If so, what could help you to do this?

*Extension activities*

Play your own variation on this game, for example;

## Handwriting race

*How to play*

Choose a sentence using every letter of the alphabet, such as 'The quick brown fox jumps over the lazy dog'. Players must see how many times they can write this sentence in a minute. The player writing most words wins. Play again to try to beat your personal record. Remember your writing must be legible!

# Word race

*How to play*

Players have two minutes to write as many words as they can think of beginning with a chosen letter, such as *j*, or combination of letters such as *ph*.

Play other mind games that rely on speed, such as

# Word pyramids

Can you build a pyramid of words, starting with one letter? How high can you build your pyramid?

*Players*:       Any number, playing individually, in pairs or groups

*Age range*:   Seven to adult

*Materials*:   Pen/pencil and paper, dictionaries (optional)

*How to play*

Players start with one letter and build a pyramid from the top to the bottom. They add a letter at each step like this:

a
at
tea
heat
heart
heater
heather

The player, pair or team building the highest pyramid wins the game. Note that letters can be rearranged, as long as each previous letter and one new letter are used each time.

1   Players choose, or are given, a letter to begin their pyramid, for example *a*.

2   Players try to build their pyramid from top to bottom as high as they can, adding one letter each time, for example:

i
it
sit
slit
stile
listen

3   The player(s) with the tallest pyramid wins.

*Questions to think about*

- Which letters of the alphabet are better for starting the pyramid game? Why?

- Are there any letters which it would be impossible to start a word pyramid from? Which letters?

- Do you prefer to play this game by yourself, with a partner or in a team? Why?

- In this game letters are used like building blocks. What else can you think of which builds up or grows like this from one thing to many things?

- Do you think that life is in any way like a pyramid? Can you give an example?

- A pyramid must rest on a wide foundation. What is a foundation? What are the important foundations in your life?

- The top or highest point of a pyramid is called a pinnacle. Are there any high points in your life? Can you give an example?

*Extension activities*

Investigate the pyramids of Egypt.

Make models of different sorts of pyramid.

Play a variation on this game, for example add-a-letter anagrams from a starter word, for example if the starter word was 'mat', words that could be made adding a letter could include – mate, meat, team, tram mart etc. Or the game can be played cumulatively, for example - mat, meat, teams, master, stammer (adding a new letter each turn).

# What if?

*Aim of the game*

The basis of creative or hypothetical thinking is the question 'What if ...?' The aim of these games is to encourage creative thinking, by thinking through the consequences of hypothetical states of affairs (see Introduction p 6)

*Players*:      Any number, playing in pairs, groups or as whole class

*Age range*:   Seven to adult

*Materials*:    Pen/pencil and paper

*How to play*

'What ifs?' provide possible starting points for discussion and writing, for example:

What if      ...plants started to walk?

...you were turned into a frog?

...people discovered the secret of eternal life?

...the oceans all dried up?

...no-one needed to go to sleep?

...you were really given three wishes?

...there were another Ice Age?

...you won a prize of £1000?

...you were given your own TV station to run?

...you discover your best friend is a thief?

What do you think would happen and why?

These or similar 'What if ...?' questions can be written on cards prior to the game, or can be written on a board during the game.

Here are some ways of playing 'What if. ...?' games.

# 1 What if – just a minute

Can you talk for one minute (or half a minute) on a given 'What if?' question?

Players play individually, in pairs or in team groups. A number of 'What if?' questions are written on cards, or on the board before play begins.

*How to play*

1  Each player, pair or team group is given, or chooses, a 'What if?' question to answer.

2  Players or teams are given a few minutes to prepare their answer, for example by brainstorming or noting ideas.

3  Each player, or representative of a pair or team of players, is then asked to speak for one minute  in answer to their 'What if?' question.

4  Players win if they can 'beat the clock' by speaking without hesitation, repetition or deviation from the subject, for one minute (or half a minute if that is their target time).

5 The discussion can then be opened to other players, to question, comment or respond to the answer that has been given. After the discussion it is the turn of the next player to answer their question and to try to 'beat the clock'.

## 2 What if – questions

Can you make up your own 'What if?' question?

How many 'What if ?' questions can you make up?

Which is the most interesting 'What if?' question?

*How to play*

1 Each player, pair or team group is asked to make up as many 'What if?' questions as they can in a given time.

2 Players, or teams, are given the agreed time to brainstorm and note down their ideas.

3 Each player, or representative of a pair or team of players, is then asked to share their 'What if?' questions. The winning players/teams are the ones who have listed the most questions, or who have reached a given target, for example ten 'What if?' questions.

*Questions to think about*

• Which do you think (from a list) is the most interesting question?

• Which is the most interesting or creative question?

• Which question(s) have you never thought about before?

• Can you think of a 'What if?' question that could *never* come about? Why?

• Can you think of a 'What if?' question that *could* happen? Why or how could it happen?

• When is it helpful for you to think 'What if ..?'

• What helps you to have new ideas?

• Is it better to have many ideas or to have one idea? Why?

• Is it useful to think of consequences of what might happen? Why?

• What is imagination? What helps you have a good imagination?

*Extension activities*

Write your answer to a "What if?' question (it helps to discuss the question first), or a poem beginning 'What if ...'

Draw the consequences of a 'What if?'

Here are some 'What if' questions to get you or your children thinking:

What if ...you were born again as an animal? Which animal would you be? Why?

...you were someone else? Who would you be?

...you had a magic carpet, where would you go?

...you could create a special day of celebration, what would you celebrate?

...there were no stars in the sky? What would you put in their place?

...you could meet someone from the past who is dead? Who would it be? What would you say?

...you could end one evil in the world, what would it be?

...you could repeat a favourite moment in your life, what would it be?

...you could create a new wonder of the world? What would it be (draw it)?

...you could have a month named after you. Which month would it be? Why?

...you could paint a message in the sky for all to see. What would it be?

...you could discover an unknown land (or planet). What would you want to find there?

## Word rules

In this simple but challenging game players try to discover a rule which links a sequence of words. The game develops awareness of the rule-governed nature of language, requiring deduction, creative thinking and the exercise of verbal intelligence.

*Players*: Any number playing as a group

*Age range*: Nine to adult

*Materials*: None

*How to play*

The leader thinks of a rule that connects different words into a sequence. Players try to guess this pattern by saying a word which follows the hidden rule. A player who discovers the rule wins.

1  A leader is chosen to think of a rule which can link a chain of words. The leader starts the game by saying the first word in the chain, for example 'apple'.

2  Players take turns to try to guess a word which could be linked to the first word, for example if the  first word was 'apple' a player might say 'apricot' (a fruit beginning with 'a"). At each turn the leader says whether the player's word follows the rule or not.

3  When each player has had a guess, the leader says another word in the series, for example 'elephant'.

4  The game continues with players guessing and the leader saying further words that follow the rule.

5  When a player says a word which does follow the rule other players have one more turn each to try to discover the rule. At the end of this round those who have said words which follow the rule must each say what the rule is. If they are right they win.

6  If the rule is not discovered within a set number of rounds, say five rounds, the leader wins. The leader repeats the sequence of words and says what the rule linking them was.

In the above example the leader had in mind the words 'apple', 'elephant', 'tomato', 'ostrich' and 'helicopter'. The rule linking the words was that each began with the end letter of the last word.

Other possible word rules are:

*alphabetical rules* eg words beginning (or ending) with same letter, next or previous letter of alphabet, alternate letters of alphabet, subsequent consonants or vowels, double consonants, an acrostic etc.

*word categories* eg words in a category such as fruit, objects of the same colour, in the same room, used for a common purpose, made of the same materials, characters from a series of books or films, ingredients of a recipe etc.

*linguistic usage* eg words derived from other languages, abbreviated words, dialect words etc.

*Questions to think about*

- What is a word?

- What is a rule?

- What rules can you think of which apply to the English language?

- Did you find it easy or hard to guess the word rules being used in this game?  Why was this?

- Do you think all words in a language follow rules? Why do you think that is?

- Could you invent a language that no-one else could understand?

- How does a baby learn a language?

- What is the best way to learn a new language?

- What rules do you have to follow in your life?

- What rules should we follow for a happy life?

*Extension activities*

Use one of the questions above for discussion or personal writing.

Write the rules of your favourite game.

Collect word rules eg what are the rules of spelling?

Create your own word rule game, for example play a 'backwards spelling' game, in which every word in a list must be spelt backwards.

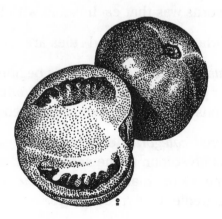

# B Logical mathematical games

## 9 Logic games

Most thinking games in this book involve the use of reasoning and logical thinking. The following games are specifically relevant to practice of logical reasoning.

### Letterlogic

This strategy game is similar to Mastermind in that it encourages logical thinking and deduction, aided by a bit of guesswork.

*Players*:      Any number, playing in pairs

*Age range*:    Nine to adult

*Materials*:    Pen/pencil and paper

*How to play*

The aim of the game is to work out your opponent's secret word by a process of logical deduction. The game is played in pairs.

1 Player 1 chooses a four letter word and writes it down without showing their opponent.

2 Player 2's task is to work out what that word is by a series of guesses and deductions. To help this process Player 1 has a set of symbols to match Player 2's guesses. The symbols are these:

✳ star = the correct letter is earlier in the alphabet

△ triangle = the correct letter occurs later in the alphabet

✗ cross = this is a correct letter in the wrong place

✔ tick = this is the right letter in the right place

Player 2 guesses the word and writes it down. Player 1 then uses the symbols to write down how close the guess came to the real letters of the word.

**3**   Player 2 wins if the secret word can be correctly worked out.

Here is an example of the game:

Player 1's word is BOAT.

Player 2 guesses SHOT and writes it down.

Player 1 places his clues under the word thus  S H O T
                                                  ✳ Δ ✕ ✔

Player 2 then guesses the correct word might be FOOT .

Player 1 again marks clues under the word F O O T
                                              ✳ ✔ ✳ ✔

Play continues until the correct answer is arrived at, or until Player 2 gives up!

*Questions to think about*

- If you got the word, what helped you to succeed in doing it?

- If you couldn't get the word, why did you not succeed?

- Is this a game of luck or of good thinking?

- Good thinking is sometimes called logic or logical. What does logical mean?

- Is all good thinking logical?

- What other kinds of thinking are there?

- What did you think or learn during this game?

*Extension activities*

Try the game with a  longer word. (It might be helpful to give a clue to the word).

Make up your own version of the game, for example with a set number of turns.

Play Mastermind. In which way is this game similar or different to Mastermind?

## Cows and bulls

Cows and bulls is a game in which players must try to find a mystery number through logical deduction and a process of elimination.

*Players*:      Any number, playing in pairs

*Age range*:    Seven to adult

*Materials*:    Pen/pencil and paper

*How to play*

1   The first player thinks of a four digit number, for example 4762, and writes it down without showing any other player.

2   The second player guesses what this number might be by saying any four digit number, for example 7234.

3   The first player must show how close this guess is by saying how many 'cows' and 'bulls' have been scored. A cow means that the guess contains a correct digit in the wrong position. A bull means that the guess contains a correct digit in the right position.

4   The second player uses this information to guess again. The first player says how many cows and bulls this guess represents.

5   The game continues until the second player has enough information to identify the mystery number.

The following is an example of play:

The first player chooses the mystery number 4762

| Second player: | First player: |
|---|---|
| '7234' | 'Two cows' |
| '4178' | 'One bull, one cow' |
| '6475' | ' Three cows' |
| '4695' | ' One bull, one cow' |
| '4726' | ' Two bulls, two cows' |
| '4762' | ' Four bulls. You've got it!' |

Paper and pencil will probably be needed by the second player to record guesses and scores, and to work out possible combinations of digits. It is also a good idea for the first player to write the mystery number down, so it is not forgotten or changed in the heat of the game.

When the mystery number is guessed players change roles and the first player must try to guess the number thought of by the second player. The player who finds the mystery number with the fewest guesses wins the game.

*Questions to think about*

- Is this an easy or hard game? What makes it easy or hard?

- Is this a game of luck or skill? Can you explain why?

- What is the smallest number of guesses you could use to win this game? Is it likely that anyone will do this? What was the smallest number of guesses used in your games?

- Is it possible to guess any number, given enough turns?

- Did you like this game? Why, or why not?

- Do you think you learn anything from this game?

- What kind of game is it? Has it a good title? What title would you give it?

*Extension activities*

Vary the rules to create your own version of the game, for example by trying to guess a five figure number, or by giving more clues.

Play other mystery number games, for example leaving mystery numbers out of given equations such as $7 \times ? = 3?$, $? \times 11 = ??$, $1? \times 4 = ?4$ and so on.


# 10  Memory Games

## Random numbers

*Players*:       Any number
*Age range*:   Seven to adult
*Materials*:   Pen/pencil and paper, display board or OHP

*How to play*

Children are told that they are going to be shown some numbers for ten seconds to see how many they can remember. No one must speak. They must look, then after ten seconds they will be asked to write what they remember on their paper. Whoever remembers the most wins the game.

1  Show the following series of numbers for ten seconds:
    1 0 0 1 0 1 1 0 0 1 0 0 1 0 1

**2** Cover the numbers and ask children to write down what they remember, without speaking or showing others their answers!

**3** Show the series and see how good they were at remembering (processing the information).

*Questions to think about*

- Was it easy or difficult to remember the numbers? Why?

- What did you think or feel when the numbers were displayed? Why?

- Did you use any strategy to try to remember the numbers?

- What helps you to remember and learn things?

- Are there any important numbers you need to remember?

- What would help you to remember these numbers?

- What did you think or learn during this game?

*Extension activities*

Try another set of binary numbers (using 0 and 1) and play another game.

Try a set of ten numerals in random order, and play the memory game.

Try remembering a set of numbers using different memory strategies eg looking carefully at the visual pattern and trying to 'picture' them in your mind (visual memory), or saying them over and over again to yourself (auditory memory), or writing them down several times (kinaesthetic memory). Which strategy do you think works best? Do they all work as well?

Try changing the length of time eg 20 seconds, one minute - does this help?

Invent your own memory games using numbers.

## Buzz fizz

*Buzz Fizz*, and the simpler versions *Buzz* and *Fizz* are good games for practising knowledge of multiplication tables. They involve players sitting in a circle calling out numbers and substituting 'Buzz', or 'Fizz' instead of multiples of a chosen number. The game calls for quick thinking and the exercise of memory.

*Players*:       3 or more

*Age range*:   Seven to adult

*Materials*:   Pen/pencil and paper

### *How to play*

For maximum enjoyment the game should be played as briskly as possible. Players sit or stand in a circle and call out numbers one after another. Players must say 'Buzz' or 'Fizz' instead of a chosen multiple. Any player who fails to do this drops out of the game.

### *1 Buzz*

The first player calls 'One', the second player 'Two', the third player 'Three' and so on. 'Buzz' must be substituted for every multiple of 5, and substituted for the digit 5 whenever it occurs in a number. Thus 5, 10, 15, 20 and so on should be pronounced 'Buzz'. If a number contains 5 but is not a multiple of 5, only part of it is replaced by 'Buzz', For example 51 should be pronounced 'Buzz one', 52 'Buzz two'.

### *2 Fizz*

In *Fizz* the forbidden multiple is seven. 'Fizz' is said for 7 or multiples of 7. The game proceeds as above, with 'Fizz' replacing 7, 14, 21 and so on, not multiples of 5 . 17 becomes '1 fizz', 27 'two fizz'.

### *3 Buzz fizz*

Buzz fizz is a combination of the two games, so that 57 becomes 'Buzzty fizz', and 75 is 'Fizzty buzz'.

A game should therefore run: '1, 2, 3, 4, buzz, 6 , fizz, 8 , 9, buzz, 11, 12, 13, fizz , buzz, 16, 1fizz, 18, 19, buzz, fizz , 22, 23, 24, buzz, 26, 2 fizz, fizz, 29, buzz', and so on.

### *Questions to think about*

- Was this game easy or difficult? Why?

- What made it easy or difficult for you?

- Does being able to think quickly mean you are good at thinking? Why?

- What did you learn from this game?

- Can you count in another language? How far can you count in that language?

- If you say a number in a different language is it the same number? Why is this?

- How many languages can you count in? How many languages are there to count in?

- Could you invent your own language or sounds to represent numbers?

- Did human beings discover numbers, or did they invent them?

- Do you think human beings thought about numbers before the spoke about them? Which came first, thought or language?

*Extension activities*

Extend the game to other combinations of numbers.

Vary the game by adding other sounds for other numbers.

Create a new sound for every digit. Can you count using our new sounds?

Invent a new design for every number, and make up some sums with them. Can others work out what digits your new number designs stand for?

Investigate how numbers are said in different languages. Can you say a multiplication table in a different language?

# 11 Number games

Number games can help develop logico-mathematical intelligence, encourage strategic thinking and give useful practice in mental arithmetic. The following are simple but rewarding number games that can be played in pairs.

## Number battle

This easy-to-play number game involves strategic thinking, mind-reading, mental arithmetic, the calculation of chances and a little luck.

*Players:* Any number, playing in pairs

*Age range:* Seven to adult

*Materials*:    Pen/pencil and paper, and a 'board' of seven circles, squares or marks in a straight line (see figure), and a small token, counter or coin.

Player A ◯◯◯◯◯◯◯ Player B

## How to play

Each player starts with 50 points. The token, counter or coin is placed in the middle circle. The aim of the game is to move the counter to your opponents' end circle.

**1** On each turn both players write down, in secret, a number of points they wish to spend. The minimum allowed is 1. When both are ready the numbers are revealed. The player with the larger number moves the counter forward one place towards their opponent's end. If the numbers are equal the counter is not moved.

**2** After each turn both players deduct the points they have used from their allocation of 50 points to give their remaining total of points. (It is a good idea for each player to check their opponent's totals before play continues!). The next turn then starts.

**3** Play continues until one player has moved the counter to their opponent's end circle, or put another way until one player has won three more turns than their opponent. If one player uses up all their points, the other can have successive unchallenged turns. If both players use up their points the game is drawn.

## Questions to think about

• Is it better to use the same number of points, each turn, or to use a different number of points, do you think? Why?

• Is this a game of chance or skill?

• What skills are involved in this game?

• Would it change the game if you had 100 points instead of 50 points? Why?

• This game is said to involve 'mind-reading'. What does that mean? Do you think you can 'read' someone else's mind?

• What mental arithmetic is involved in this game? Do you have any rules of your own that you use to help you add up or take away?

• What is the smallest number of points needed to win a game?

*Extension activities*

Investigate variations on this game.

Invent your own number battle games, with boards and rules of your own devising.

## Fifteen

The aim of this game is to be the first player to make a total of fifteen out of three numbers.

*Players*:      Any number, playing in pairs

*Age range*:    Seven to adult

*Materials*:    Pen/pencil and paper, or cards numbered 1-9 and
                counters.

*How to play*

This game starts with a row of nine squares or cards labelled one to nine.

1  Players take it in turns to choose one square or card per go.

2  The winner is the first player to occupy three squares (or take three number cards) which add up to fifteen.

*Questions to think about*

- Did you find this an easy or hard game? Why?

- How many different ways are there of making fifteen with these nine cards (estimate first then work out the answer)?

- Does it matter who starts first? Why?

- What is the best strategy for winning the game?

- Can you think of any questions whose answer is fifteen?

- Did you enjoy this game? Why, or why not?

- What did you think or learn during this game?

*Extension activities*

Make up as many questions as you can which have the answer 'Fifteen'.

Invent another number game using the same nine number cards.

Invent another number game using different number cards and rules, for example 'Twenty five':

## Twenty five
*How to play*
This game uses a set of cards or squares numbered 2-15

| 2 | 3 | 4 | 5 | 6 | 7 | 8 | 9 | 10 | 11 | 12 | 13 | 14 | 15 |

The players take turns to pick up numbers.

The first to have numbers that add up to 25 is the winner.

## Up to a hundred
*Players*:      Any number, playing in pairs
*Age range*:    Seven to adult
*Materials*:    Pen/pencil and paper

*How to play*

1  The first player writes any number from 1 to 10 on a piece of paper.

2  The next player writes a second number from 1 to 10, and adds the two numbers together.

3  Players go on taking turns in choosing a number from 1 to 10 and adding it to the running total.

4  The player who adds the number to the total to make 100 is the winner.

*Questions to think about*

• Can you think of a strategy to help you win every game?

• Would it be a different game if the target number was fifty, or another number?

• Does it matter who goes first? What is a fair way of choosing who goes first?

- Is this a game of luck or skill?

- What would make this a better game?

- Is 100 an important number? Why, or why not?

- Can you think of anything that exactly numbers 100?

*Extension activities*

Invent your own variation on this game.

Investigate ways of making 100 using all the digits 1–9 and mathematical symbols.

Count up to 100 in a different language.

Find out ways of saying or writing 100 in different languages.

Write as many questions as you can with the answer 100.

## Countdown

A co-operative number game that encourages perseverance in problem solving. This game has no winners or losers. Everyone wins who completes the countdown.

*Players*:       Any number, playing in pairs

*Age range*:    Seven to adult

*Materials*:    Pen/pencil and paper, and counters or cards marked 1 to 9

*How to play*

Begin with cards or counters marked 1 to 9, and three columns marked on a board or piece of paper. The aim of the game is to get all nine numbers in a single column in a countdown order ie 9-8-7-6-5-4-3-2-1, with 9 a the top and 1 at the bottom.

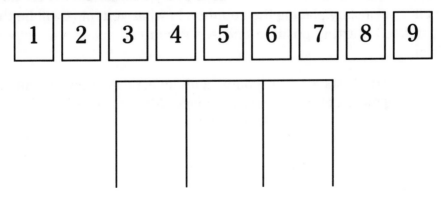

1 Shuffle the counters face down, and place three counters face down in each column.

2 Turn the counters placed in each column number side up, ready to play.

3 Players take turns to move on a counter at a time from the bottom of one column to the bottom of another column.

Note: A counter can only be moved under a lower number. When a column is empty any of the bottom counters can be placed at the head of it, as the rule about being under a larger number cannot apply.

There is a way out of every position no matter how stuck you seem!

*Questions to think about*
- What is a number?

- Where in life do you see the numbers 1–9 in order?

- How many different ways are there of ordering the digits 1, 2, 3, 4, 5, 6 ,7, 8, 9?

- This game is a puzzle. What is a puzzle?

- What is a problem? Is there a difference between a puzzle and a problem?

- Does this game teach you anything about problem solving?

- Is there an answer to every problem? Why, or why not? Can you give examples?

*Extension activities*

Test the claim that there is a way out of every position no matter how difficult it seems, by placing the counters in what you think will be the most difficult starting position and see if you can achieve a winning position.

Work out variations on the game, and investigate how it can be extended eg more columns, more numbers, different rules?

# Count out

This is one of many number games better played with a calculator.

*Players*:        Any number, playing in groups of twos, threes or fours

*Age range*:    Seven to adult

*Materials*:     A calculator for each player, or pen/pencil and paper

*How to play*

1   Two, three or four players key a secret three digit number into their calculators (and write them down on paper).

2   Players take turns to ask their neighbour for a number from 0–9.

3   If that player has that digit as part of his calculator number he must declare the number and deduct it from his total eg a 5 in a total of 150 would represent five tens or 50, which he would declare and deduct from his total leaving 100 as the new total.

4   The player who correctly identifies the number adds it to his total ie in the example above adds 50 to his total.

5   Players take turns until one player has won all the points, and the others are left with nought.

Note: Writing the original numbers down before the game helps to prevent arguments later!

*Questions to think about*

• Is it better to ask for a high number or low number? Why?

• What is your definition of a high or low number?

• Does it make sense to ask for the same number more than once? Why?

• Are you more likely to win the higher your starting number? Why?

• Is this a game of luck or skill? Why?

• This is a a game you can play with a calculator. What is a calculator?

•  In what ways are you similar to, and different from, a calculator?

*Extension activities*

Try playing a variation on this game eg with four or more digits.

Can you invent your own calculator game involving secret numbers?

## Secret number

A 'mind-reading' game which encourages logical deduction and develops numerical understanding.

*Players*:       Any number

*Age range*:   Seven to adult

*Materials*:    None

*How to play*

1   A child volunteers to think of a secret number between 0 and 100.

2   The rest of the group have ten questions to try to discover the secret number.

3   The child with the secret number can only answer 'Yes' or 'No'.

*Note:* With a younger child a limit of 100 might be best, or up to 10,000 with older students. It is a good idea if the child writes down their secret number on a piece of paper, to prevent possible changes of mind during the game.

*Questions to think about*

• Was it easy or hard to guess the secret numbers? Why?

• Are some numbers harder to guess than others? Why, or why not?

• (Before the game) How many questions do you think it will take to guess the secret number?

• (During the game) What question will best help us to narrow down the possible number of answers?

• (After the game) What strategies best guarantee that the number can be found in under ten guesses?

• Is this a game of luck or skill? Why?

• Do you like numbers? Why, or why not?

*Extension activities*

Adapt the game to find a mystery animal, or any object - investigate strategies for finding the answer with the smallest number of questions.

See also 41 'Twenty questions' p 41.

# Estimation

Human judgement is developed by practice in making judgements, and by skill in evaluating those judgements against the opinions of others and the availing evidence. Estimation is a game which encourages players to make numerical judgements as estimations of given amounts. The game involves estimation, approximation and judgement according to evidence.

*Players*:     Any number, as individuals or pairs

*Age range*:    Seven to adult

*Materials*:    Different materials with which to make estimations of measurement (examples given below), pen/pencil and paper

*How to play*

The aim of the game is to challenge players, individually, in pairs or small groups to make estimations of a range of different materials such as a jar half filled with beans, a length of ribbon, a large pat of butter, a book, a bowl of cornflakes, a tube of sweets, a glass of water, a shirt, a brick, a cushion and so on. It is a good game for pairs of players as this allows for conferring. The winners are the ones who can most accurately estimate the correct given measurement.

1  Show the players an object which they must judge and estimate in terms of a given unit of measurement, for example the number of beans in a jar, how long a piece of string is or how heavy a brick is. One minute is allowed for judgements and conferring to take place.

2  Players write their estimated measurements on their paper, and are then presented with their next challenge, for example how many grams in a pat of butter or bag of flour, how many pages in a book, or how high the ceiling is. They are given a minute for each estimation.

3  The true measurements are revealed eg by counting out the beans, measuring the string etc. Players check their estimations to find out who was nearest in estimating each object. The winners are those whose estimations are the best for each category. A further round may be played by each of the winners facing a final challenge to find the overall winner.

*Questions to think about*

- Does it help in making estimations to work with a partner? Why, or why not?

- Do you make better estimations the longer you think about it?

- What helps you make better estimations?

- What in life do you have to estimate?

- Is there a difference between an estimation and a guess? What is the difference ?

- What would help you get better at estimating things?

- If we played this game again do you think it would help you get better at making estimations? Why?

*Extension activities*

Create your own estimation game eg invite players to suggest, or bring in, examples of objects for estimation, or cut pictures of priced objects from a shopping catalogue to estimate prices.

Discuss how you might measure things if you had no measuring instruments to help you.

Research measurement in the past.

Collect pictures of real objects eg the Eiffel Tower, a flea or a famous person, to estimate and find the measurements of.

Using an atlas, map or globe estimate and measure distances between one place and another. How far are you from Paris? Are you nearer New York or Cairo?

Body maths – list different parts of your body to estimate and measure eg how many pulses can you feel in a minute, how heavy your head is, the length of each toe.

Can you estimate the passing of a minute's silence?

See also the estimation game Steps p 162.

# Grab

This is an estimation game in which a player picks a number of objects from a pile, and scores according to the number of objects that have been taken. The game helps in the practice of multiplication and division, as well as in exercising judgement about numbers.

*Players*:        Any number, playing individually or in pairs, in groups of four

*Age range*:   Seven to adult

*Materials*:    A heap of small objects such as buttons, beans or stones; pen/pencil and paper

*How to play*

A pile of more than 200 small objects is placed between the players. Each player grabs a handful of objects in turn and then  calculates their score as follows:

2 points if you can make sets of 2 objects with no remainder

3 points if you can make sets of 3 with no remainder

4 points if you can make sets of 4  with no remainder

5 points if you can make sets of 5 with no remainder

For example a player picking 8 objects would score $8/2 = 4$ (2 points), $8/3 = 2r2$ (0  points), $8/4 = 2$ (4  points), $8/5 = 1r3$ (0  points). Total = 6 points.

1   Each player in turn grabs a handful of objects from the pile.

2   Players count how many objects they have taken.

3   Players score  2 points if divisible by 2, 3 points if divisible by 3, 4 points if divisible by 4 and 5 points if divisible by 5.  They record their score.

4   Each player in turn takes another handful of objects to add to their pile, and score again as above, adding the points to their score.

5   Players can play a third or more rounds, if they have sufficient in the pile for every player on each turn to take some objects. The winner is the player or pair with the most points.

*Questions to think about*

• Is it better to pick a small number or large number of objects? Why?

• How many would you  want to try to pick to get a high number of points?

- What number of objects would give you the highest number of points?

- What is the highest and lowest score you got? How did this happen?

- What does this game help to teach you?

- Is it a good game? Why?

- Could the game be improved? How?

*Extension activities*

Vary the game, for example by increasing the range of numbers to divide into the total, to include 6, 7, 8, 9 and so on.

Play estimation games by grabbing piles of objects. Can you estimate how many you pick up? Can others estimate how many you have picked up?

## Target

A card game that provides useful practice in handling numbers and a context for mathematical thinking and discussion.

*Players*:       Any number, playing individually or in pairs

*Age range*:   Seven to adult

*Materials*:    Playing cards with court cards removed, or number cards, pen/pencil and paper

*How to play*

The game is played with an ordinary pack of cards with the jacks, queens and kings removed, giving a pack of 40 cards. Aces count as 1. Alternatively forty cards in four sets numbered 1–10 could be used. As each player needs five cards for a game, up to 8 players can play with one pack of cards. Players win if they can make a target number from five cards that are dealt to them.

Before the game starts a *target number*, any number up to 100, must be chosen. The target can be chosen in various ways, for example players can take turns to choose the target number, or the number can be chosen randomly by opening a book and using the page number or choosing two cards (the first card gives the tens digit, the second the units digit, so that a  3 and 8 gives 38, a ten card counts zero).

1   Each player is dealt five cards, and must try to combine some or all

of them to make the target number. For example with the cards 1, 3, 5, 6, and 9, a target of 38 could be made by (9 x 3) + 5 + 6.

2   Players who can make the target number with any or all of their card numbers (plus mathematical symbols) show their cards and explain how they make the target.

3   Any player who can make the target scores the target number of points.

4   Any player who cannot make the number is given another card. If the target number can now be made the player scores half the target number of points.

5   If a player still cannot find a combination to make the target number another card is dealt. If the target number can now be made the player scores a quarter of the target points.

6   When everyone has played a  new hand is dealt, and the scores added on.

7   After an agreed number of hands the winner is the player with most points.

*Questions to think about*

•   What might be different ways of choosing the target number? What do you think is the best way?

•   What kind of game is this? How would you describe it? Is it like any other game?

•   Do you prefer to play by yourself or with a partner? Why?

•   Did you find this an easy or a hard game? Why? What was easy or hard about it?

•   Is it a useful game to play? How might it be useful?

•   Did you enjoy playing the game? Why?

•   What do you think would be a hard target number to get? Why do you think so?

•   Have you found any target number that was impossible to get in five cards? Do you think there is an impossible number? Do you have a reason for thinking so?

•   What does it mean to 'have a target'?

•   Do you have any targets in your life?

*Extension activities*

Create your own card game using the numbers on cards, for example:

## Line Up

A game for 2 or 4 players, using a pack of 40 cards as above.

*How to play*

In this game 36 cards are laid out in a 6 x 6 square. Two of the remaining cards are shown, which added together give the target number. Each player tries to spot and grab two cards which add up to the target number. The player who picks up most cards wins. Play later rounds with 3 cards for the target number, and then 4 cards.

# 12  Probability games

The assessment of probability is a skill needed in maths, in science and in all aspects of living. The following games provide opportunities to develop skill and awareness of probability as the calculation of chances. They invite players to think critically in exercising their judgement.

## Spoof

Spoof is well known as a pub game, used for deciding who should buy the next round of drinks. It is a simple game which requires the calculation of numerical chances, and the use of strategic bluffing. The probabilities involved are as much psychological as mathematical.

*Players*:      Any number, playing in groups, ideally in fours

*Age range*:   Seven to adult

*Materials*:    Counters or other small objects such as beans

*How to play*

The aim of the game is to make an informed guess at the total number of counters concealed in the hands of the group. The winner of each round drops out. The loser is the last player left in the game. The skill of the game comes in calculating what the total might be, and in 'spoofing' or bluffing others about the number of counters you have in your hand.

**1** Each players in the game has three counters. If there are four players there are 12 counters in the game.

**2** Each player puts three counters in their hands, puts their hands behind their backs or under the table, and puts any number of counters from 0–3 in their playing hand. They keep any remaining counters in their other hand out of sight.

**3** When each player is ready they put their playing hand as a closed fist in front of them on the table.

**4** Each player, playing clockwise, then says how many counters in total they think are in all the hands on the table. No two players may guess the same number.

**5** Players then open their hands to show how many counters they have. The number of counters is added up and the person who correctly guesses, or is nearest the number wins.

**6** The winner drops out and the remaining three players play again, making a new fist with a chosen number of counters from 0–3 in their playing hand. The person sitting clockwise to the left of the player who guessed first last time has the first guess of each new round. The game proceeds as above.

**7** In the final round only two players are left. The person guessing correctly, or is nearest the correct number, wins. The remaining player is the loser.

*Questions to think about*

- What is a 'spoof'?

- Why is this game called 'spoof'?

- Was there spoofing going on in your game?

- Who do you think has the best chances of winning, the person who guesses first, or last, or does everyone have an equal chance?

- Is there any strategy that could help you win or do you win just by guessing?

- Is this a game of luck or skill, or both? Can you explain why?

- Is what happens in your life a matter of luck or skill?

*Extension activities*

Create your own variation on the game, for example by varying the number of players or the number of counters.

Hold a Spoof competition to find the overall winner or loser in your class.

Play other bluffing games such as 'Call my bluff' (see p 23).

# Pig

Pig is a  simple dice game that calls for the assessment of probability.

*Players*:       Any number

*Age range*:   Seven to adult

*Materials*:   Pen/pencil and paper, and one die

*How to play*

The winner is the player to reach an agreed score, for example 50 or 100.

1   The order of play is decided by each player throwing the die once. The player with the lowest score begins the game.

2   Players take turns to throw the die and score the points shown on the die. A player may throw the die as many times as they like, each throw adding points to the score, until they decide to stop. But if a one is thrown it ends the turn and the player's whole score for that turn is lost.

3   Players take turns throwing the die until they throw a one or decide to stop, and record their scores. The player to reach the target score is the winner.

The player who begins has an advantage. One way of evening the advantage is for all the players to have the same number of turns. The player with the highest score is then the winner. In this game the last player has the slight advantage of knowing what score to get to win. The fairest way to play is to organise it as a series of  games in which each player in turn has the chance to play first.

*Questions to think about*

•   Is the order of play important? Which player or players, if any, do you think have an advantage? Why?

- What way of playing would give every player the same chance of winning?

- Were you lucky or unlucky during your game? Why do you think so?

- What do you think is the best strategy in throwing the die to win the game?

- What is the probability of throwing a one with an ordinary die?

- Suppose you had thrown a 6, a 5, a 4, a 3, and a 2. What would be the odds that your next throw would be a one? (Answer: the probability remains 1 in 6 no matter what numbers have been thrown before.)

- Is it probable that in every six throws you would throw a one? How could you prove this?

- There is an old saying 'the die is cast'. What do you think it might mean?

*Extension activities*

Vary the rules to create your own dice game. Show the game to others and discuss strategies for playing the game.

Investigate dice of different kinds and shapes.

Play the game 'Twenty five' (p 94) using a die.

## Cat and mouse

Cat and mouse is a race game in which a cat tries to catch a mouse. The mouse is given a start. What is the probability of the cat catching the mouse? Will the mouse escape down its hole in time, or will the cat catch the mouse?

| | |
|---|---|
| *Players*: | Any number, playing in pairs |
| *Age range*: | Seven to adult |
| *Materials*: | Pen/pencil and paper, counters or objects to represent the cat and mouse, dice |

*How to play*

The aim of the cat is to catch the mouse. The aim of the mouse is to reach its hole. The cat wins if it catches the mouse. The mouse wins if it reaches its hole. Players in the game try to predict which will be the winner.

1 Draw a race track twenty squares long. The cat begins at square one, the mouse begins at square ten. Square twenty is the mouse hole.

2 The cat or mouse moves according to the number thrown on a dice. If the number is 1, 2, 3 or 4 the mouse moves that number of spaces towards the hole. If the number is 5 or 6 the cat moves that number of spaces towards the mouse. Before the game starts players predict who will win, the cat or the mouse.

3 Players take turns to throw the dice, and to move the cat or mouse according to the number shown,

4 If the mouse reaches square twenty, or beyond, it is safe and has won the race. If the cat reaches the same square as the mouse, or beyond, the mouse is caught and loses.

5 The players who were correct in their prediction win the game.

*Questions to think about*

- Why did you predict the cat or the mouse would win?

- Which is more probable at the start of the game - the cat or the mouse to win?

- Can you explain why the cat or the mouse should win?

- Could you change the game to give better chances to the cat or the mouse? What would give them better chances?

- How true to life is this game?

- What other animals, apart from a cat and mouse, could this game be about?

- Are there any other games you know like this game?

- Is there anything in your life that is a matter of chance like this game?

*Extension activities*

Vary the rules of the game, for example by changing the distances the cat and mouse have to move, or the numbers for cat and mouse on the dice.

Create your own version of the game, for example 'Tortoise and Hare' which is played as follows:

# Tortoise and hare

*How to play*

Tortoise and Hare, represented by counters or objects, start side by side on square one and must reach square twenty to win. The tortoise moves when number 1, 2, 3 or 4 is thrown, the hare moves when 5 or 6 is thrown on a dice.  Can you predict who will win? Why do you think so? Investigate other ways of playing Tortoise and Hare.

# Red or black?

A strategy game involving assessing probabilities, predicting outcomes and making decisions. The game is a version of 'The prisoner's dilemma' (see below), a famous problem in moral philosophy and in the mathematics of decision-making or game theory.

*Players*:      Any number, playing in pairs

*Age range*:    Seven to adult

*Materials*:    Playing cards, or cards marked with a black or red symbol on one side, Pen/pencil and paper

*How to play*

1   Players sit facing a partner.

2   Each player is given two cards, a red card (any red playing card) and a black card (any black playing card). They can look at these cards.

3   At a given signal each player chooses a card (red or black) to play, without showing or telling the other player which card has been chosen.

4   The players show each other their chosen card.

5   Players score the result depending on what cards have been played.

If two red cards are played each player scores 3 points.

If a red and black are played, the black scores 5 points, the red scores minus 2 points.

If two black cards are played each player scores 0 points.

After the rules and scoring have been explained, and a trial round played, the game should be played in two rounds, as follows:

# Red or black: competition

In the first round each player tries to score the highest points for themselves as possible.

The teacher organises the competition so that each player plays every other player in turn, and each player's score is recorded after each game.

When all the players have had a turn at playing each other, or after an agreed number of games, the individual scores are totalled. The winner is the person with the most points.

After the competition, invite the players to review the strategies they used during the game. The following are some questions to consider:

- What did you think while you were playing?

- What strategy did you use to play?

- What do you think is the best strategy to win most points? Why?

- Did you play the same strategy against every player? Why?

- Do you think you could get a higher score next time you played? Why?

# Red or Black: co-operation

In the second round the players try to score the highest number of points for the whole group.

As before each player plays every other player in turn, and the each player's score is recorded after each game.

When all the players have had a turn at playing each other, or after an agreed number of games, the individual scores are added to create a score for the whole group.

Compare the total score of the group from the individual competition with the total score from the group co-operation round. Which game made the higher individual and whole group scores?

After the competition invite the players to review the strategies they used during the game. The following are some questions to consider:

*Questions to think about:*
- What did you think while you were playing?

- What strategy did you use to play?

- What do you think is the best strategy to win most points for the whole group? Why?

- Did you play the same strategy against every player? Why?

- Do you think you could get a higher group score next time you played? Why?

- Which do you prefer, a game where you compete with others or co-operate with others? Why?

- What did you like or not like about this game?

*Extension activities*

Discuss the nature of games, inviting children to respond to questions such as:

- In what ways is life like or unlike a game?

- Do you think life has, or should have, rules?

- What does 'co-operation' and 'being selfish' mean?

- Can you think of any examples of real-life dilemmas that people may face?

This game is a version of the famous decision-making problem called 'The prisoner's dilemma'. The central dilemma in the problem is : Is it better to behave selfishly or co-operatively? The story is as follows:

You and your criminal partner have been caught by the police after committing some crime. You are taken to separate rooms to be questioned. The police say they have enough evidence to send you both to jail for a year, but not enough evidence to send you to jail for longer. But if you confess to your crime, and say your partner was also involved, you will be let free for co-operating with the police and your partner will go to jail for three years. If you both confess, then the police will not need your co-operation, and you will both go to jail for two years. You are told your partner will be offered the same deal. What would you do?

It is a dilemma because looked at one way you are better off confessing, but looked at another, you are better off not confessing. The alternatives can be shown on a table :

|       | Red   | Black  |
|-------|-------|--------|
| Red   | 3/3   | –2/+5  |
| Black | 5/–2  | 0/0    |

Note: The term 'game theory' was invented by the Hungarian mathematician John von Neumann (1903-1957), who argued that many real-life situations were like games. A 'game' for von Neumann was any situation in which there were competing interests, and in which everyone was trying to maximise their profits or benefits. Many of life's games, in the political, economic or personal sphere, he thought were like the 'prisoner's dilemma' in which we must decide whether to act selfishly or co-operatively, assessing how others will act and react to what we do.

# 13  Shape games

## Pentominoes

Pentominoes is an abstract board game, good for visual thinking and developing understanding of spatial relationships. It was invented more than forty years ago by mathematician Solomon Golomb.

*Players*:     Any number, playing in pairs

*Age range*:   Seven to adult

*Materials*:   A set of pentominoes (these can be bought but it is easy enough to make your own out of card, or for children to make them as part of a mathematical investigation), a chessboard.

*Note:* The pentominoes should be made of squares which are the same size as the squares on the chessboard.

A set of pentominoes

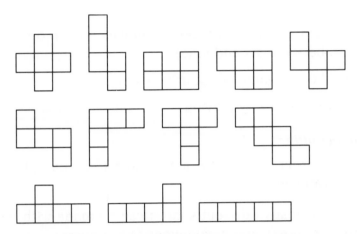

Pentominoes are made up of all the different shapes that can be made by joining five squares together, so that each touches along the edge of another, and no edges overlap.

## How to play

Two players need a set of twelve pentominoes and a chessboard on which to play. The object of the game is leave your opponent no place on which to move.

1  Players decide (eg by spin of a coin) who plays first. If more than one game is played the  loser should start the next game first.

2  The first player places one pentomino on the board, exactly covering five squares on the chessboard.

3  The next player chooses one of the remaining pentominoes and places it on five vacant squares of the board. At no point should any pentomino overlap another.

4  Players take turns until there is not enough room for one player to fit one of the remaining pentominoes. The player who cannot fit a pentomino on the empty spaces of the board loses.

## Questions to think about

• What is a square? Where do you see square shapes?

• Why are these shapes called 'pentominoes'? What does 'penta' mean? Are there any other words which begin with 'penta'?

• Can all twelve pentominoes be fitted onto the board? (The answer is yes, but children can have fun investigating this).

- How many pentominoes can *you* fit onto the board, without any overlapping?

- What is the average number of moves in an ordinary game? (Answer: between six and nine).

- Did you like this game? Why, or why not?

- What did you learn by playing this game?

*Extension activities*

Play with a partner to see how many moves you can play in a game (play co-operatively).

Investigate how many different shapes can be made with tetrominoes (sets of four squares), and hexominoes (six squares).

What shapes can be made with four (or more) equilateral triangles?

What shapes can be made with three or more hexagons?

Investigate each pentomino in turn. Can you describe one (without showing your partner) to see if your partner can identify it from your description?

Note: for more on the mathematical investigation of polyominoes see *Investigating Maths* Book 2 pp 20/21 (R. Fisher & A. Vince, Stanley Thornes).

# Shapely drawing

Players are asked to copy a geometrical drawing which they cannot see, with the help of members of their team. The game involves skills in giving and following directions, and practice in mathematical imagery and use of language.

*Players*: Any number, playing in two teams

*Age range*: Seven to adult

*Materials*: Pen/pencil and paper for each player, large paper or board and markers, pens or chalk

*How to play*

With more than 6 players the game can be played in two teams, with less than 6 the game is best played individually or in pairs. The game involves players trying to copy a simple, non-representational geometric drawing. The drawing can be prepared beforehand by the leader (in which case omit Stage 1) or be the first stage in playing the game, as follows;

Stage 1: *Preparing the drawing*

1 The contents of a simple geometrical drawing are chosen by the leader or by the players, for example; 1 square, 2 triangles, 1 circle and four straight lines.

2 Each player makes a drawing using these elements.

Stage 2: *Copying the drawing*

1 A copier from each team leaves the room.

2 The leader, or selected player, chooses one drawing to be copied. It is placed where the players, but not the copier, can see the drawing.

3 The copiers return, and on a large piece of paper, white or black board, try to reproduce the drawing from instructions given by players in their team.

4 Team members from each team take turns in giving the copier instructions. A player can give as many instructions as they wish on a turn and both copiers can make use of the information given.

5 A player must stop giving instructions when the copier makes an error. An error cannot be corrected until another team member has a turn.

6 The first copier to completely reproduce the drawing wins.

*Questions to think about*

• Did you find this game easy or difficult? Why? What made it so?

• Was it easier to be the copier or one giving instructions? Why?

• Did you find some things in the drawing very difficult to describe?

• Did you find it difficult to imagine in your mind's eye what a drawing being described was like?

• What would help you be better at this game? Would you get better at it with practice?

• What do you think of this game? Does it teach you anything or help you think in any way?

• The game involves geometrical drawing. What makes something 'geometrical'?

- Are there some shapes you cannot describe in words?

- Are there some things you cannot describe in words?

- Are there any things that you could not imagine, even if they were described to you?

*Extension activities*

Vary the drawing game to include other subjects (see p 131 for more drawing games).

Collect and display geometric pictures, paintings and designs from artists and designers.

Hold a geometric design competition, with players trying to produce the best-designed geometric drawing from given elements, allowing the drawing to be coloured or painted.

## Topology

Maze games are topological games which rely on logical thinking and the processing of visual/spatial information. They are to do with exploring space and shape through being set problem solving tasks, using geometrical properties and relationships to solve problems. The following is a maze games that sets visual and topological challenges. This game was invented by an American professor of economics called Gale.

*Players*:      Any number, playing in pairs

*Age range*:   Seven to adult

*Materials*:    Pen/pencil and paper, or prepared game board

*How to play*

You need to draw a game board as follows:

```
   X   X   X   X   X   X
 O   O   O   O   O   O   O
   X   X   X   X   X   X
 O   O   O   O   O   O   O
   X   X   X   X   X   X
 O   O   O   O   O   O   O
   X   X   X   X   X   X
 O   O   O   O   O   O   O
   X   X   X   X   X   X
 O   O   O   O   O   O   O
   X   X   X   X   X   X
```

The objective of the game is to get from one side of the board to the other either left to right (the 'o' file) or top to bottom (the 'x' file). The obstacle is that the other player is trying to get across or down, and will be trying to block you. The winner is the first player who crosses the board.

1  The players choose to play along either the x-files or the o-files.

2  The player on the o-file goes first, and joins together two neighbouring o points with a straight line.

3  The player on the x-file joins any two neighbouring x points together with a straight line.

4  Players take turns to join any two of their adjacent points together. The only rule to remember is that lines must not cross.

5  The winner is the first player to make an unbroken line across the board. The o-player must get an unbroken line from left to right, the x-player from top to bottom.

The winning line will probably snake all over the board. This is an example of a winning game for the x-player:

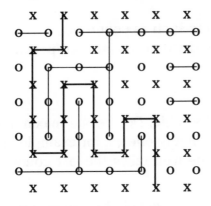

*Questions to think about*

- Is there an advantage in going first? Why?

- Would you say the person who goes first always, usually or sometimes wins? Why do you think so? Can you prove it?

- Can there ever be a draw in this game? (No, because the only way one player can stop the other winning is to win).

- Is there any advice, or strategy, for helping somebody to win?

- Do you know what the word 'Topology' means?

- What kind of game is this?

- Did you think this was a good game to play? Why, or why not?

*Extension activities*

Can you invent a game of topology using different rules?

Can you invent a game of topology using a board of your own design?

Collect examples of mazes and create your own maze puzzle.


# 14 Strategy games

## Take the last

A simple game which encourages children to think about strategies needed to win, and aims to encourage logical and strategic thinking.

*Players*:        Any number, playing in pairs

*Age range*:    Seven to adult

*Materials*:     A collection of small objects such as counters, matchsticks, beads, coins, dried beans etc. Pen/pencil and paper

*How to play*

Put a single pile of small objects on the table. Decide the maximum number that can be taken from the pile in any one go, for example up to 10. The winner of the game is the one who takes the last counter from the table.

1  Decide who is to have the first turn, for example by agreement or toss of a coin.

2  The first player takes from the pile any number of counters up to the agreed maximum.

3  Players take turns to remove counters (one or more, up to the maximum) from the pile.

4  The player who takes the last counter is the winner.

*Questions to think about*

- Can you describe what happened in your last game?
- Is there a way of winning each time?
- Can you think of a strategy to win each time? (Try working backwards from the problem.)
- How many counters do you estimate you have in your pile?
- Does it matter how many counters are in the pile to begin with?
- Is this a game of luck or skill? Why?
- What did you think or learn while playing this game?

*Extension activities*

1 Try reversing the game so that the player who takes the last match is the loser. Investigate winning strategies for this game.

2 Work out strategies for games in which different numbers of counters are taken.

The following games are variations on 'Take the last':

# Poison

Another simple game to encourage logical and strategic thinking.

*Materials:*    Ten counters, matchsticks, blocks or tokens, or pen/pencil and paper

*How to play*

Two players have ten counters or tokens between them (or they draw them on paper). Players can take one or two from anywhere in the row. The last counter left is 'poison'. The player who is left with it is the loser.

1 The first player takes one or two counters from the row.

2 The second player does the same. Players take turns to pick up one or two counters.

3 The player who is left with the poison (the last counter) is the loser.

'Take the last' games can help develop a number of problem-solving skills and strategies including prediction, planning, trial-and-improve methods, making and testing hypotheses, looking for patterns, proving and disproving, and working backwards from a problem. Working backwards from a problem can be helpful if children find it difficult to identify a winning strategy. Children may discover how to win every time if they are guided through the following strategy:

'If you leave one for your opponent you win. If you leave two who will win?' (Your opponent, by only taking one). 'If you leave three who may win?' (Your opponent if s/he takes two). 'What if you leave four?' (You will, because your opponent will have to leave two or three).

The player who leaves four or seven should win every time. Then ask, 'Who should start the game, if you want to be sure to leave seven?' (Your opponent. If s/he takes one, you take two; if s/he takes two, you take one - and you should win every game!)

*Questions to think about*
- If you could only take one each time who would win?
- If you could only take two each time who would win?
- In this game, if you had eight left how many would you take to win?
- Can you work out a way to win every time?
- Does it matter if you play first or second?
- What happens if you begin with fewer counters?
- What happens if you begin with more counters?
- What happens if you choose to take three counters each time?

*Extension activities,*
Invent your own rules for a game of Poison.

Play a variation on the game of 'Poison' such as 'In line', 'Nim' or 'Tactix' as follows:

# In line
*How to play*
In this game players can take one or any two counters but only if they are next to each other.

1    Place any number of counters or matches (up to 20) in a line.

○○○○○○○○○○○○○○○○○○○○

**2**  Decide whether the person who takes the last match is the winner or loser.

**3**  Players take turns to take either one match or two (if they are next to each other).

**4**  The winner – or loser – is the one who takes the last match.

What is the winning strategy? What variations on this game can you create?

## Nim

*How to play*

Nim is a more sophisticated strategy game, made famous in the film *Last Year in Marienbad*. Its name comes from the German word *nimmt* (take). The game is usually played by two players but can be played by partners or group teams.

**1**   Place counters or matchsticks in this formation:

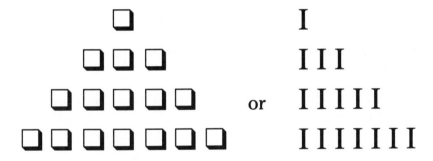

**2**   Players take turns to take one or more counters from any one row.

**3**   The loser – or winner – is the person who picks up the last counter.

Can you work out a winning strategy? Can you create a variation of the game, varying the number of rows or number of matches, and number of matches that can be taken on each turn? Share your game with others and explore winning strategies.

## Tactix

*How to play*

A variation on Nim in which the counters are laid in a square or rectangular formation, for example:

☐ ☐ ☐ ☐

☐ ☐ ☐ ☐

☐ ☐ ☐ ☐

☐ ☐ ☐ ☐

Players take turns to take any number of counters they like from any one row or column, vertically or horizontally, but the counters must be next to each other. For example in this formation only the first two can be taken (as there is a gap in the row) or the last one:

The loser is the player who picks up the last counter.

What is the winning strategy? Can you create your own problem-solving game?

Can you explain how 'Take the last', 'Poison', 'In line', 'Nim' and 'Tactix' are different from each other?

# 15  Strategy board games

Board games have been played in every culture throughout human history. All board games which do not simply rely on luck require strategic thinking and can become the subject of critical thinking and discussion. Even simple board games which require only pencil and paper can provide interest and cognitive challenge.

The following are some simple board games requiring visual/spatial and strategic thinking, to play, think about and discuss.

# Three in a row (Achi)

Achi is an African version of noughts and crosses (tick-tack-toe).

*Players*:       Any number, playing in pairs

*Age range*:   Seven to adult

*Materials*:    Pen/pencil and paper, eight coins or counters

*How to play*

1   Draw a board of this design:

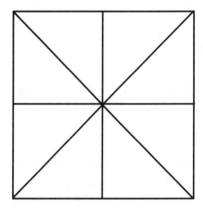

2   Two players have four counters each.

3   They take turns to place one counter on the board.

4   When all the counters have been placed on the board, players take turns to move a counter to a vacant spot. They must move if they can.

5   The winner is the first to get three counters in a row vertically, horizontally or diagonally.

# Nine men's morris

*How to play*

This is one of the oldest board games. Boards like the one below have been found carved on a slab in an Egyptian temple (c. 1300 BC). Evidence of the game has been found at a Bronze age burial site in Ireland, in ancient Troy and Viking Norway and in medieval Europe.

The board for Nine Men's Morris consists of three concentric squares connected by lines. The aim of the game is to reduce all your opponent's men to two, or to block your opponent so that further moves are impossible.

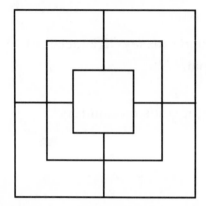

*Players*:      Any number, playing in pairs

*Age range*:   Seven to adult

*Materials*:   Pen/pencil and paper, or playing board with 9 counters for each player

*How to play*

Two players have nine counters, different colours for each player, which they can place on any of the 24 points (intersections) of the board. The object is to make a row of three. Each time this is done a player may remove one of the opponent's pieces. A player wins when their opponent is blocked or has only two pieces left and so cannot make a row of three.

1   In part one, players take turns to place their counters one at a time on the board

2   In part two, players take turns to move one of their counters along a line to a vacant point, to try to make a row of three.

3   When a row of three is formed ie three counters along a line vertically or horizontally, the player can remove one of the opponent's pieces.

## Three men's morris

*How to play*

This is a simpler version of Nine Men's Morris played on a board with nine points. Players have four counters each and aim to get three in a row.

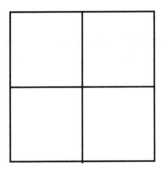

In the cathedrals of Norwich, Canterbury, Gloucester, and Salisbury, and in Westminster Abbey there are boards cut into the cloister seats, perhaps to relieve the tedium of long services!

## Avoid three

In this game the object is not to get three in a row. The player who gets three in a row loses the game.

*Players*:      Any number, playing in pairs

*Age range*:   Seven to adult

*Materials*:    Pen/pencil and squared paper, or chessboard with pawns/draughts/counters, or pegs and pegboard

*How to play*

1   Players take turns to place a piece or counter on the board.

2   A player loses the game when he plays a piece to make a line of three, vertically, horizontally or diagonally.

(On an 8 x 8 chessboard there can never be more than 17 moves because the largest number of pieces that can be placed on a chessboard without having three in a line is 16.)

Challenge: can you place eight pawns, draughts or counters on a chessboard so that no two are in line vertically, horizontally or diagonally?

# Go

Getting a number of pieces in a row is the basis of Japan's national game Go. This game was invented in China about 3000 years ago, making it the oldest board game still regularly played today. The game is as strategically complex as chess. This is a simplified version that still requires strategic thinking and planning.

The aim of the game is to make a row of five, vertically, horizontally or diagonally, and to block your opponent's attempts to do the same.

*Players*:      Any number, playing in pairs

*Age range*:    Seven to adult

*Materials*:    Pen/pencil and squared paper

*How to play*

Go is one of the oldest strategy games in the world, thought to have originated in China about 2000 BC. The traditional Go board is a ruled square with 19 horizontal and 19 vertical lines, and players have 100 white pieces or 'stones' or 100 black pieces each. This simpler version, called Go-muku in Japan, is played on squared paper, and the aim is to get five of one's own colour or symbol in a row, horizontally, vertically or diagonally, and to prevent the other player from doing so.

1  Players choose different symbols eg letters, and play on squared paper.

2  Players take turns to draw their symbol in any empty square.

3  The first player to make a line of five is the winner. If no-one succeeds in forming a line of five the game is drawn.

*Questions to think about*

- Is Go a game of luck or does it need thinking about?

- Go is called a game of strategy. What is a strategy?

- Did you have a strategy to help you win while playing this game?

- Does the player who plays first have an advantage?

- Do you think you could get better at playing this game? How could you get better at playing it?

- This is a game where players try to capture territory (squares). What other games do you know which are like this one? Give an example. In what ways is it like or unlike this game?

- Did you enjoy playing this game? Why, or why not?

- Does this game help develop your thinking? If so, in what ways? If not why not?

*Extension activities*

Invent your own game using this board but with different rules.

Create your own game using a board of a different design.

Find and display a Chinese or Japanese picture showing people playing Go.

Invite and interview a person who has a real Go board and pieces.

Research and investigate board games from around the world.

## Aggression

Aggression is a strategy game in which players attack and conquer each other's countries. It is a simple but complex game, that can offer challenge to children and to professors of mathematics.

*Players*:      Any number, playing individually or in pairs

*Age range*:    Nine to adult

*Materials*:    Pens or pencils of different colour and a large piece of paper

*How to play*

A playing area needs to be drawn on a large sheet of paper. One player begins by drawing the boundaries of an imaginary country. Each player in turn then draws the outline of an imaginary country which joins to one or more of the other countries up to the agreed number of countries in the game. Any number of countries can be drawn, but 20 is a good number, with fewer, perhaps 10 for younger children. The countries can be any shape or size.

Figure 1 is an example of countries that have been drawn ready to play.

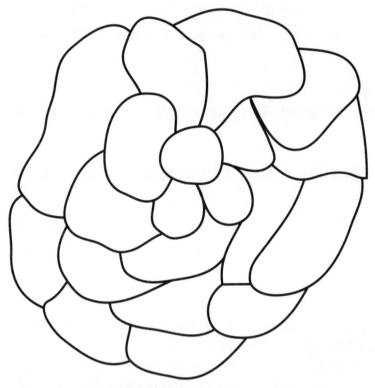

*Figure 1: Drawing the boundaries*

Each player has 100 armies (or 5 armies for each country in the game) which when the game begins he will place in whatever country he chooses.

1  Players have a playing area of an agreed number of countries, such as 20 (as in diagram above).

2  Players take turns to occupy countries with a number of armies. They occupy one country each turn with as many armies as they wish, and write that number in the chosen country (using pencil or pen of different colours). A player may decide to occupy a few countries with many armies, or many countries with a few armies. This stage of the game ends when each player has used up all their armies, or when no countries are left to be occupied.

Figure 2 illustrates all 20 countries occupied in a game (player 1 indicated by numbers in circles, player 2 by numbers in squares.

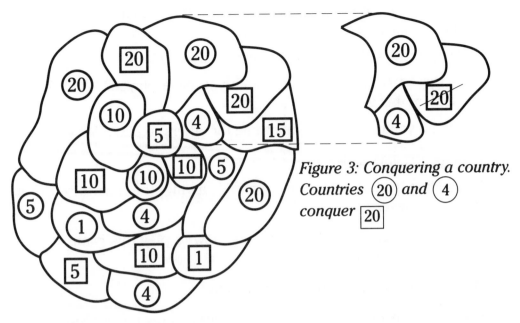

Figure 3: Conquering a country.
Countries (20) and (4)
conquer [20]

*Figure 2: Positioning the armies*

**3** The third stage of the game is the aggressive part. Each player takes it in turn to occupy a country which is occupied by the other player's army. A country can be occupied only if the player's armies in adjacent countries outnumber the armies of the occupying player. The number of armies in the conquered country is crossed out and they take no further part in the game. If a country is not occupied by either player it takes no part in the game, and is declared 'neutral'. Figure 3 shows a country being conquered.

**4** The game ends when neither player can conquer any more of the other player's countries. The player occupying the highest number of countries is the winner.

*Questions to think about*

- Why is this game called 'Aggression'? What is aggression?

- Is it a good title for the game? Why, or why not?

- Is it an easy or hard game to play? What makes it easy, or hard?

- How did you decide where to put your armies?

- Do you think it better to put your armies far apart or close together?

- Do you think it is better to have  many armies in a few countries or a few armies in many countries?

- Do you think this game is like life in any way?

- Is this game like any other game you have played? What do you think of this game?

- Would you recommend this game for others to play?  Why?

*Extension activities*

Investigate games which involve occupying the territory of the opposing player.

Write a set of rules to show someone how to play this game, or your version of this game.

Design a flag and/or medal for your army.

Create a mime or play showing the causes and results of aggression.

Discuss an occasion when you saw or were the perpetrator or victim of aggression.

# C   Visual, Spatial and Kinaesthetic games

## 16  Drawing games

Drawing games exercise visual intelligence. They develop thinking by encouraging the translation of the visual into the verbal and *vice versa*.

### Artist

How good are you at visual thinking? Can you see things in your 'mind's eye'? Can you do a drawing from another person's description? In this game the players are artists who must try to draw from another's description.

*Players*:      Any number, playing in pairs or groups of 4 to 12

*Age range*:   Seven to adult

*Materials*:    Large sheets of drawing paper, coloured pens, pencils or crayons and paper

*How to play*

Players can play this game in opposing teams or as one co-operative group. For this game a number of drawings or coloured pictures are needed. Each player chooses a picture from either:

- a pack of art resources

- a collection of magazine pictures

- a drawing done by each player, using a large sheet of drawing paper and coloured pens, pencils or crayons on which to draw the picture.

The chosen or drawn picture is not shown to any other player. The pictures are placed in a pile face down ready for the game to begin.

1  One player in the group is chosen to be the 'artist', and is given a blank sheet of drawing paper, and some pens, pencils or crayons to draw with.

2  The artist sits on the floor with all the other players sitting behind in a semi-circle.

3  One of the prepared pictures is placed behind the artist so that the other players can see it.

4  Players take turns in giving the artist directions, instructions and advice on drawing the unseen picture. The aim is for the artist to try to draw the picture as similar to the original as possible. For example if the picture was of a house the first player might say, ' Draw four lines to make a box'. The next might say: 'Draw a door on the middle of the bottom line of the box.' The next: ' The house has a triangular roof ...' and so on.

5  When the players have finished giving advice, the two pictures are compared. The artist chooses someone from the group to become the next artist for a new drawing.

*Questions to think about*

•  Could you visualise a picture in your 'mind's eye' when it is described to you?

•  Are some kinds of picture easier to visualise than others?

•  When you compare the pictures were there any parts of the original drawing that the players had forgotten to mention?

•  Do you think you learn anything from this game?

•  How could this game be improved?

•  Do you think you are a good artist or good at drawing or not? Why do you think so?

•  How could you become better at being an artist or someone who can draw?

*Extension activities*

Play the game using simple geometrical designs. Are they easier to describe and to copy? (See 'Shapely drawing', p 114)

Play a variation on the game, for example 'Drawing race':

## Drawing race

*How to play*

One player is leader, the other players form two or more teams. The leader writes the name of an object on each of five slips of paper, eg cat, house, radio, umbrella, telephone. Identical sets are prepared for each team. When the leader signals, a player from each team runs to see the first slip of paper held by the leader, then back to the team to draw whatever object is named on a piece of paper. As soon as someone in the team correctly identifies the object being drawn, it is written on the drawing and returned to show the leader, who then reveals the next object to be drawn. The first team to identify all the drawn objects wins the game. In other rounds more complex and challenging objects can be chosen for the drawing race.

## Squiggles

One of the key aspects of creative thinking is elaboration, that is the ability to take a small beginning and to extend it in many, varied and unusual ways. Squiggles is a game which challenges players to elaborate on a visual theme.

*Players*:     Any number, playing as individuals in pairs

*Age range*:   Seven to adult

*Materials*:   Pen/pencil and paper, or board markers and white or blackboard

*How to play*

The aim of the game is to make the most original, interesting and unusual drawing possible from a given squiggle. A squiggle drawing is a quick sketch or any small mark on the drawing paper or board which becomes the starting point for the drawing. When played as a competition between two players, as below, the winner is the more creative drawing as judged by an umpire or by popular vote.

1  An identical or near-identical squiggle (small shape, curve or line) is drawn on two large drawing surfaces such as two halves of a blackboard or large sheets of paper.

2   Two contestants are given identical drawing tools, and are given time to study and think about the drawing they will develop from the squiggle.

3   At a given signal the two players start drawing. Their drawings must extend from or include the original squiggle. After a set time, from 2–5 minutes, or when both have finished, the drawings are ready for display and judging.

4   A judge who does not know the author of each drawing may be invited in to judge which is more creative. Or the judgement may be made by the popular vote of the whole group.

5   The person who wins may be invited to draw the squiggles for the next contestants.

*Questions to think about*

•   Can you visualise a drawing from a given squiggle, or does a drawing just develop as you draw?

•   Can you learn or practise anything useful in this game? Does it help you in any way?

•   What is a good drawing?

•   What criteria would you use to judge a finished drawing?

•   Do you always prefer one drawing to another? Why?

•   Why do you think early peoples such as cave dwellers began drawing in the first place?

•   Can drawing help you think or learn? How, and when?

*Extension activities*

Hold a squiggle drawing exhibition.

Hold a speed drawing competition using different genres eg portraits, still lifes, seascapes, skies etc.

Invent your own creative drawing game, for example 'Blindfold drawing':

# Blindfold drawing

*How to play*

Two players volunteer for a blindfold drawing contest to take place using chalk and blackboard or felt pens and whiteboard or large paper. The players are blindfolded and given something to draw with and a drawing surface. They are given the subject for a drawing by the leader, for example, a self portrait, their house, their school, a cow, a vase of flowers etc. The blindfold artists each try to draw the subject as best they can. When they have both completed their drawing they stop, and remove their blindfolds. Other players vote for the drawing they think is better, and the drawing with the most votes wins.

# Multiple masterpiece

A game similar to Squiggles but played as a team effort to create a joint masterpiece, or at least a creative group picture.

*Players*:       Any number, playing in groups of 4-6

*Age range*:   Seven to adult

*Materials*:     Coloured pens, pencils or crayons and large sheets of
                 paper

*How to play*

Teams of 4–6 players have a set of drawing tools and a large sheet of paper. There may be two or more teams. At a given signal they begin to create a joint masterpiece, as follows:

1   One person begins each team picture by drawing a squiggle ie a basic shape or outline. Each team has the same squiggle shape to begin with.

2   The first player adds a few more strokes, the next does the same and so on in turn – but players must obey the rule that *every time they add something to the picture they must make it look like something quite different.* No speaking or communication about the picture being created is allowed.

3   The joint masterpiece is completed when no member of the team wishes to add anything more to the picture.

4   The winning picture may be judged and chosen by a referee or by non-participating players.

*Questions to think about*

- What title would you, or your group, give to your joint picture? Why that title?

- What did each member of the team visualise the final picture would be like?

- Did you like working as part of a group? Why, or why not?

- What might be the problems of doing a group picture? Did you have any problems in your group?

- Did the game make you think or help you to understand anything about art?

- What is a masterpiece? Can you find an example of a masterpiece? What makes it a masterpiece? Would everyone agree it is a masterpiece? Why?

- Does calling something a masterpiece mean it must be by a man? Is it a good word to use? Why?

*Extension activities*

Play the same game using other materials such as paint, collage, montage etc.

Create a team drawing game, for example 'Multiple portraits':

## Multiple portraits

*How to play*

The game is played in teams of 4–6 players. At a given signal each player must draw the portrait of someone in the room. Teams should be given a few minutes before the start to decide who they will draw and to ensure no-one in the team draws the same person. At the end of a time limit, say ten minutes, each team displays their joint portraits. A judge, or non-participating player, is asked to make one guess to identify who was the subject of each portrait. The team with most correctly identified portraits wins the game.

## Abstract drawing

A simple visualisation game, moving between the abstract and the representational in perceiving and drawing shapes. Players try to make marks which do not look like an object while the group, or opposing players, try to identify an object in the marks.

*Players*:      Any number, two or more playing

*Age range*:   Seven to adult

*Materials*:    Pen/pencil and paper, chalkboard and chalks, or markers and whiteboard

### How to play

1  Each player takes turns to make a simple mark on the board such as a line, a curve, or a squiggle. As each player makes their mark in addition to the drawing they should make sure their mark shows nothing recognisable as an object.

2  Once four or more marks have been made players may look for something in the drawing.

3  If a player sees something they can call out 'Stop!', say what they can see and trace the object on the board to complete the drawing. The player wins if judged by other players to have traced something recognisable.

4  The winning player rubs the board clean and begins a new game with a single mark.

### Questions to think about

- Did you think this was an easy or hard game to play? Why?

- This game involves trying to draw an abstract picture. What does 'abstract' mean?

- Do you prefer drawing abstract or representational pictures? Why?

- Was it easy to visualise something from the drawings being done in the game?

- Is it possible to make an abstract drawing that reminds you of nothing, or does every drawing remind you of something?

- Is there anything good, bad or interesting about this game?

- Did you think or learn anything during this game?

*Extension activities*

The game can be played in pairs, with players taking turns in making marks. When one player sees and traces a recognisable object from the drawing they win that round and one point. Five points wins the game.

Create your own abstract drawing game, for example 'Mystery pictures':

## Mystery pictures

*How to play*

This game is an adaptation of the Rorschach Blot Test (illustrated in *Teaching Children to Think* by R. Fisher, p 52). Each player makes an ink or paint blot on one half of a large piece of paper, folds it over and presses down. When the paper is opened up it should reveal an abstract shape. These pictures are left to dry and are numbered. The game consists of players (in pairs or teams) having one minute to look at each mystery picture and to write down as many things as the picture makes them think of. The leader could introduce the game by saying: 'What titles could you give each picture?' Each picture is viewed and titles listed. No title or words in titles can be used twice. At the end of the game one point is given for each title, provided a reason can be given by the player if challenged to justify the title. The player or team with the most points wins.

## Quick on the draw

This game requires speed of thinking in creating and drawing original ideas based on a number of simple recurring shapes. It encourages productive thinking - the creation of many, varied and unusual ideas in a short space of time.

*Players:*      Any number, playing individually or in pairs

*Age range:*    Seven to adult

*Materials:*    Pen/pencil and paper, prepared pages of basic shapes

*How to play*

The aim of the game is to invent different drawings based on the same circle shape within a set time. Marks are awarded for the number of different ideas, and for originality of ideas.

1  Players are given pages of circles (each about 4 cm diameter) and

are told that on a given signal they must draw as many different things as they can within a set time, say ten minutes, each drawing based on one circle. They should write underneath what each drawing represents eg face, sun, watch, spider's web etc.

2 At the end of the game players share their drawings, and score 1 point for each different idea they have drawn, and 2 points for each idea which no-one else has drawn.

(For a visual illustration of circle drawing see *Teaching Children to Think* p 48)

*Questions to think about*

• How many possible drawings could be invented from a circle?

• Do you prefer to work with a partner at this game or by yourself? Why?

• Which do you think is more important to have, many ideas or a few good ideas? Why?

• Are you good at thinking of ideas in this game?

• What do you think your best idea was?

• What did you learn from this game?

• Is it fair that people who have ideas that no-one else has thought of should get more points in the game? How many more should they get? Why?

*Extension activities*

Play the same game using sheets of different shapes eg triangles, squares, rectangles, ovals, letter shapes, number shapes, symbol shapes (see also Shapely drawing p 114),

Invent your own drawing game based around shapes, for example 'Plate design':

# Plate design

*How to play*

Players will need a cardboard plate, and paints. Players are either given a theme, such as the sea, flowers, their town, the seasons, a local festival etc. or are given a free choice. They paint their own design onto their card plate within a given time, say 20 minutes. Allow more than one plate each, in case of mistakes. Display finished designs when dry, and ask someone to judge the winning designs.

## Design time

Creative thinking is shown by an unusual and original response to a given situation. The following game exercises this ability by calling for interesting uses for a common object.

*Players*:        Any number, playing individually or in pairs

*Age range*:   Seven to adult

*Materials*:    Pen/pencil and paper, a common object such as a cup, T-shirt or umbrella

*How to play*

Players are asked to think of as many ways as they can of improving a common object, and to draw their ideas. In this game marks are awarded for fluency and originality of ideas.

1   Players each have pens or pencils and paper. They are shown a common object such as a plain white tea cup, and told to think of as many ways as they can to improve the design of the object within a given time. They draw their designs and write underneath what they have shown eg add a hat, paint a smile, put it on wheels etc.

2   After the game designs are shown and discussed. A point is given for each different idea, and two points if no other player has had the same idea.

*Questions to think about*

• What was your best, or most creative idea?

• What was the best or most creative idea which someone else had?

• Do you prefer to play this game, think of designs, by yourself or with a partner? Why?

• What did you learn from this exercise?

• Could you make a model of any of the designs? Which one would you choose to make a model of?

• Designers and inventors patent their ideas. What does this mean?

• If you have a good idea and write it down it becomes your own intellectual property. What does this mean?

*Extension activities*

Collect and study examples of the range of designs of a chosen common object such as teapot, sports shoe or lunchbox. Discuss which you think are the best designs and why.

Think of other common objects you could improve by your own design, such as litter bins, pen holders or your bed. Make a display or exhibition of your designs.

Design your own coat of arms, with symbols that represent your own life and experience, or your own flag.

Create your own creative design challenge. The following is an example of an 'Improve it' challenge – to improve the human body:

## Improve it – the human body

*How to play*

Players are given paper and pencil and told to design and draw some improvement or improvements to the human body. At the end of a given time, say 15 minutes, each player shows their drawing and explains what improvements they have designed. Players may then vote to find out whose design was thought to be the most creative and original.

# 17 Memory games

## Kim's game

Kim's game is named after the hero in Rudyard Kipling's book *Kim*. Part of Kim's training was to sit cross-legged on the floor in front of a low table covered by a cloth while his teacher arranged coloured stones, beads and other objects of different size, shape and colour on the cloth. After a short while the display was covered and the boy was asked to remember everything he had seen, not only what he had seen but the position of each object related to the other objects. A variation of this game was to send the boy out of the room and rearrange the objects, removing some, adding and replacing others, then challenge Kim to say what had been changed. These games could be reproduced, starting with a few items and working up to the recall of more complex combinations.

*Players*:     Any number, playing in pairs

*Age range*:   Seven to adult

*Materials*:   A tray, a piece of cloth, and a varied selection of common items

### How to play

Ten common objects are placed on a tray and covered over with a large cloth.

1   The objects on the tray are shown to players for one minute, before they are covered up or the tray taken away.

2   Each player is then given a minute to see how many items they can recall. This can be done through verbal recall or by asking players to write down (or draw) the objects they can remember.

3   The player wins who can remember most objects.

### Questions to think about

• Was it easy or difficult to remember the items on the tray? Why?

• Did you use any strategy to try to remember what items were on the tray?

• What would help you to remember things more easily? Would concentrating on the shapes or initial letters help you to remember?

• Do you have a photographic memory? How many things can you visualise at any one time'?

• How do you think your memory works?

• In what ways would being better at remembering things be of help to you?

• Did you think this was a good game to play? Why, or why not?

### Extension activities

Vary the number of items to make it more challenging eg try 12 or 15 items.

Play Kim's other game of altering the arrangement of objects, removing and replacing some, and see if players can see what has changed.

Vary the time allowed for looking at the objects. Does giving a shorter or longer time for looking alter the player's ability to recall the objects correctly?

See also the memory observation games on p 88.

## Memory pictures

Memory mixes elements of Kim's Game and Suitcase. It uses instead of objects a numbered list of pictures that players must try to commit to memory.

*Players*:      Any number, good for larger groups

*Age range*:    Seven to adult

*Materials*:    Pen/pencil and paper (optional)

*How to play*

Collect ten pictures, numbering them from one to ten.

1  Show the pictures in numbered order to the group who must observe them carefully.

2  After showing the pictures, say any number from one to ten. The first player to tell you what the picture is that corresponds with the number is the winner and scores a point. (Alternatively all the group try to write what the picture is and all who identify it correctly get a point).

3  After each round say the next number, and see how many can remember all the pictures.

4  After reading all the numbers on the list, make a new list and start again, this time reading the numbers in random order.

5  Any player who can recite, reconstruct or remember the list of pictures in their original order wins the game (or a lot of points!).

*Questions to think about*

(See 'Kim's game' above)

*Extension activities*

Ask children to make their own collection of pictures for the Memory picture game around a particular theme.

Ask children to choose a poem to memorise, and to share or record at a later date.

See the story and discussion plan on memory in *Stories for Thinking*, in this series, p 77.

## Pelmanism

Pelmanism is a memory game played with a pack of cards. Traditionally playing cards are used, but any picture, word or symbol cards would work.

*Players*:       Any number, playing in small groups

*Age range*:   Seven to adult

*Materials*:    A set of illustrated cards, or pack of playing cards

*How to play*

1   Lay the set of cards face up for all to see, then turn them face down.

2   Players take turns to choose a card, name or describe the card, and turn it face up to see if they have correctly identified it.

3   If they have correctly identified the card they keep it, and can choose again from the face down cards. If they identify a card wrongly it is turned over again.

4   Players take turns until all the cards are taken. The player with most cards correctly identified wins the game.

*Questions to think about*

(see questions on memory games above)

*Extension activities*

Play other memory observation games with cards, for example place a group of cards in a particular sequence on the table or floor, ask players to hide their eyes or turn around, change some of the cards and see which players can spot the difference.

Play Pelmanism with other kinds of cards, such as number cards and with a collection of pictures such as postcards.

Play Pelmanism as a 'turn over the pairs' game, asking players to identify two cards (pairs) at a time. Extend the challenge in other rounds by asking them to identify and turn over three or more cards.

# 18 Miming games

## Mime the word

This is an entertaining game in which players attempt to guess what adverb is being mimed. The game challenges both miming and language skills.

*Players*:     Any number

*Age range*:   Seven to adult

*Materials*:   None

*How to play*

It is a good idea to prepare, or for the players to brainstorm, a list of adverbs before the game so that players have a number to choose from when the game begins. A player mimes an adverb for the others to guess. They can ask for the player to mime an action in the manner of the word. The player who guesses the adverb wins a point. If no-one guesses, the miming player gets a point.

1   The first player chooses an adverb such as quickly, happily, quietly, angrily, bravely, carelessly, proudly, nervously, dreamily, grumpily etc.

2   The other players in turn ask the first player to carry out an action in the manner of the word, for example 'eat like this', 'laugh like this', 'look like this' or 'clean your teeth like this'.

3   The first player must mime the word as the player asks, and the players may make a guess at the word as soon as the acting begins.

4   The first player to guess the word wins a point. If no-one guesses it after each player has had a chance to ask for an action, the miming player wins a point.

5   When each player has had a turn at miming a word the player with most points wins.

*Questions to think about*

- The game involves miming adverbs. What kind of word is an adverb?

- What is a mime? Is it the same as acting?

- What can you, and what can't you communicate through a mime?

- Are there any feelings that you cannot show through mime?

- Can you tell what people are feeling by looking carefully at them? Give examples.

- What can you learn about people by looking at them?

- Some people use their hands, faces and bodies a lot when talking to others. Why is this?

- Are there some words that you cannot mime? Can you give examples of any?

- What would be the hardest thing to mime?

- When is miming useful? Are you good at miming? How could you get better at it?

*Extension activities*

Create a mime of a famous story in groups. Can others guess the story?

Mime a story while someone is  reading it out.

Create a mime to a piece of music.

Play a variant on the game, for example miming verbs, prepositions or adjectives, or vary the roles by playing 'Act the word':

## Act the word

*How to play*

The first player leaves the room while the others decide what word they will act, for example slowly, sadly, cautiously, guiltily, enthusiastically, loudly, longingly, desperately, slyly, stupidly etc. When they have chosen the word the first player returns and asks them in turn to do an action in the manner of the word, for example 'Read a story like this' or 'Comb your hair like this'.  The  actions can involve speech, gesture and facial expression. The first player can try to guess what the word is after every action, and wins if the guess is right. If the word is not guessed after each has performed an action, the other players win.

# What's my line?

*Players:*     Any number, playing individually or in teams

*Age range:*   Five to adult

*Materials:*   None

## How to play

Players take turns to pretend to have a particular job or occupation, such as nurse, window cleaner, actor, reporter, teacher, car mechanic etc. which the rest of the group or team have to discover by asking questions of the player acting the mime which can only be answered 'yes' or 'no'.

1  The player chosen, or volunteering, to begin the game chooses an adult job or occupation to mime to the rest of the group.

2  The group has to discover what this mystery occupation is by guessing or by asking questions that demand a 'yes' or 'no' answer. They may ask for the mime to be repeated once more.

3  The player who discovers the correct occupation wins. If the occupation is not discovered the player doing the mime wins. A player wins only if the mime fairly represented the occupation, the occupation is a real one and no-one has guessed it.

4  The winning player may nominate who has the next turn.

## Questions to think about

• Are there some occupations that cannot be shown in a mime?

• What are the easiest, and most difficult, occupations to mime?

• Are there any differences you would show if you were miming a man or a woman doing the same occupation?

• What are the differences, and similarities, between speaking and miming?

• Is miming a way of communication with others?

• Is miming a kind of language? If so, what kind of language is it? If not, why not?

• Are there some things you cannot communicate through mime? What, and why?

- Are some people better at communicating through mime than others? In what ways are some mimes better than others? Can you give an example?

- Is miming a useful skill to have? Why?

- Are you good at miming? Why do you think so? How could you become better at it?

*Extension activities*

Extend the game by miming an accident during the course of the occupation.

Brainstorm a list of occupations. Categorise these occupations into sets of your choosing.

Invent your own game based on 'What's my line?', for example 'What's my game?'

# 19  Music games

Music, like a game, follows its own rules, and has its own game pieces or instruments with which to play. Music appreciated for its own sake is a universal human capacity. Music is made by being played not only on instruments but also in the mind. It is perhaps a uniquely human form of intelligence. The following game aims to help develop musical intelligence.

## Paper music

Paper music challenges players to make music using only a sheet of newspaper, in co-operation with others in a group. The game includes four processes – composing, performing, responding to, and hopefully understanding more about the nature of music.

*Players*:      Any number, playing in groups of 4–6

*Age range*:    Seven to adult

*Materials*:    Pages from a newspaper

*How to play*

The aim of the game is for each group to plan, practise and perform a piece of 'music' using only sheets of a newspaper as musical instruments. Each group should consist of four to six players, and a wide selection of newspaper pages should be available for experimenting with. Players are put into groups before the game starts.

1  Each player chooses or is given a sheet of newspaper. They may use other sheets if they need them.

2  Players experiment in making sounds with their sheets of newspaper. They may tear, fold, crumple, roll, or use the paper in any way they wish to make different kinds of sound. Some ways of making sound include waving, flicking, crumpling, tearing, blowing, beating, stamping on, pulling along different surfaces.

3  The group of players puts together their different sounds to make a piece of continuous music. They practise their music (writing it down using their own form of notation if they wish), ready to perform it to others.

4  Each group gives a title to their finished piece.

5  At an agreed time each group performs their piece of paper music.

*Questions to think about*

• What is music?

• What makes sounds music?

• Were the sounds that you made with paper in your group music? Why, or why not?

• What are the differences between newspaper and other instruments such as the violin, xylophone and drum?

• How many different kinds of sound did you make? How would you describe these sounds?

• What difference does it make if you play loud or soft, slow or long?

• How did you choose the title for your piece?

• Why did you choose that title?

• What did you learn from playing 'Paper music'?

*Extension activities*

Compose paper music to a given title, such as Storm, Rain, Thunder and lightning, Sea sounds, Beach scene, Windy day, or Moonlight.

Investigate how many different sequences of sounds you can make in your group with the same set of sounds. Choose which sequence sounds best. Discuss why you think so. See what others think.

Draw or paint a picture to suit your paper music composition.

Write a story or poem to go with your paper music.

Create a dance or mime to go with your paper music.

# Bell ringing

In this game a group of players become a peal of bells, and try to create a musical composition from the sounds they make. The game calls for co-operation, creative thinking and the exercise of musical intelligence.

*Players*:      Any number, playing in groups of about six

*Age range*:   Nine to adult

*Materials*:    Pen/pencil and paper for notating bell ringing sounds (optional)

*How to play*

Players in each group create a  sound by saying a word like 'dong' or 'bong'. They try to remember their special sound by repeating it and comparing it with the sounds made by other members of their group. They try to order their sounds from high to low, thus creating a range of musical sounds with which to compose a  piece of music. The group can practise a known tune like 'Happy Birthday' if they like but the aim of the game is to compose a piece of music that has never been heard before. Time is given for this. *Each player is only allowed to make one bell ringing sound.* Groups may notate the music in their own way if they wish, for example by numbering the players' sounds. Groups perform their compositions at the end, and the best composition is judged the winner.

1   Players in their group begin by creating their own bell ringing sound. They are allowed to make only one sound with a word like 'dong' or 'bong'.

2   Each group agrees what sound each player will make. The aim of

the group is to create a range of sounds so that an interesting piece of music can be made with the sounds.

3   Groups are given time to practise their bell ringing sounds and to put them in order from high to low.

4   Groups now try to compose an original  piece of music with their sounds. Each player is allowed to make only one note, but these can be repeated in any order, and at any speed. A group may wish to appoint a conductor to compose the music, for example by pointing at players when they are to make their sounds. Groups may write their music down in any way they wish. This has the advantage that it can be played again and altered and is kept in permanent form. A title should be given to each piece of music that is composed.

5   When all groups are ready they perform their music to each other. The compositions may be judged to choose a winner. If there are several groups their compositions can be played one after another to create a bell ringing symphony!

*Questions to think about*
- Why is this game called 'Bell ringing'?
- What was easy and what was difficult about this game?
- Were you able to compose an original  piece of music?
- Did you give your music a title? Why did you give it that title? Is it a good title? Why?
- Did you compose your music as a group or did a person do it for you?
- In what ways was this game musical?
- How many different bell ringing sounds could be made, do you think?
- Could you write down the musical sounds you made? How might this be done?

*Extension activities*
Play the game using percussion or tuned instruments.

Listen to two different kinds of unaccompanied singing, such as Gregorian chants and folk songs. Discuss which you prefer and why.

Paint or draw a picture with the same title as your, or a chosen, piece of music.

# 20 Observation games

Visual thinking depends on developing the skills of close observation. The following are games which encourage close and thoughtful observation.

## Spot the difference

Players in this game must observe, think and remember carefully enough to detect slight changes in the environment.

*Players*:      Any number, playing individually or in two teams

*Age range*:   Five to adult

*Materials*:    None

*How to play*

Spot the difference can be played in a number of ways. The following version is particularly suitable for young children and played in two teams. The team scoring most points wins.

1   Players form two teams which face each other.

2   Team A looks carefully at all players in Team B and tries to notice everything about them.

3   Team A leaves the room, while each member of Team B changes at least one thing about themselves (for example players may exchange shoes or jewellery, remove a sweater or glasses, undo a button or shoelace, put a pen in a pocket, tuck in a shirt or leave it hanging out, and so on).

4   Team A returns to the room, faces Team B and in turn tries to spot one difference in any member of Team B. One point is awarded for each change that is noticed.

5   Team B now looks carefully at Team A, leaves the room and so on as before.

To play this game with a class or large number of children divide them into three teams, with the team not playing offering ideas and exchanging various articles with the playing team, allowing all children to be involved, and more variation and challenge in the game.

*Questions to think about*

- Do you find it easy or difficult to spot the changes? Why?

- What was the hardest or easiest change to spot?

- What helps you to remember what you see? Are you good at seeing things in your 'mind's eye'?

- Do you think if you played this game often you would get better at it? Why?

- Is this a good game to play? Why?

- Is it useful to have a good memory? Why?

- Is it useful to be able to spot changes in things? Can you give an example when it is useful?

- Are there people who have jobs in which they must be good at observing and noticing differences in things?

- Are there any subjects you study at school in which it is helps to be observant?

- How observant are you? Why do you think that? Can you give an example?

*Extension activities*

Create your own 'Spot the difference' game, for example using pieces on a chessboard, the arrangement of items in a doll's house.

Collect some examples of 'Spot the difference' picture competitions from comics etc.

## Observation board

*How to play*

Players draw an 8 x 8 grid representing a draughtsboard (or are given graph paper). The leader arranges a number of white and black pieces randomly on a draughtsboard, without showing the players. When all are ready the draughtsboard is revealed for ten seconds, during which time the players must try to memorise the positions of the pieces. The board is then hidden and players fill in their own grids showing what they think is the correct pattern of the pieces. Players score one point for each piece they place correctly on their grid. By varying the number of pieces for each round the leader can make this a challenging and stimulating game. Other games boards and pieces could also be used for this game.

## Book check

This is a simple game that tests players' powers of observation, memory and knowledge about books.

*Players*:        Any number, playing individually or in pairs

*Age range*:    Seven to adult

*Materials*:     Pen/pencil and paper

*How to play*

The game can be played individually but is more interesting played in pairs. Players are given time to look at a book before being asked questions about features of the book to test how much they have observed and can remember. The players with the highest number of correct answers wins. The leader will need to select a book tailored to the age and interests of players, and prepare some questions before the game starts.

1    Choose a book that the players are not likely to have read, and pass it round telling them to take a good look before passing it on. Players should be allowed one minute to study the book.

2    When everyone has had a chance to see the book the players are set a series of questions, between ten and twenty, to see how much they observed and can remember from looking at the book. The following are examples of questions you might ask:

Who was the author of the book?

What was the title of the book?

How many pages were in the book?

Was there a picture on the cover?

Was the book illustrated?

How many chapters were in the book?

Was there a price on the book?

Was it a fiction (story) or non-fiction (information) book?

3    Answers can be given by players in turn, with the question opened to other players if a wrong answer or no answer is given; or the first player with hand up can be chosen to answer the question.

4 One point is given for every correct answer. The game may have a number of rounds, with different kinds of books being inspected. The players with most points win the game.

*Questions to think about*

• What was easy to remember and difficult to remember in the Book check game?

• What were you asked about that you had not observed while looking at the book?

• How many questions were you able to answer correctly about a book?

• Were there some things about the book you observed but were not asked a question about?

• How many questions do you think you could ask about a book? Give examples.

• What people need to know a lot about books? Why do they need to know about books?

• What have you learnt during this game?

• Would you call yourself an observant person? Why?

• Would being good at observing and remembering things be helpful to you? How might it be helpful?

• What would help you be better at observing and remembering things?

*Extension activities*

Players can be asked to select a book for the game and prepare some questions about it.

Invent a variation on the game for example using several books at a time, or using other forms of printed material such as magazines, food packets, a map book or Yellow Pages.

Play an observation game using artefacts or objects, such as 'Mystery objects':

## Mystery objects

*How to play*

The leader collects some interesting objects to use in the game. One object at a time is placed behind a screen so that none of the players can see it. The first player comes out to look at the object, and then must describe it (without naming the object) to the rest of the players, who are allowed three guesses as to the identity of the object. The player who identifies the object can have a turn at describing the next mystery object. (A variation of this game is to place the mystery object in a bag and let the players feel the mystery object in the bag before guessing what it is.)

# 21 Problem-solving games

Human beings are problem-solving animals. Though physically vulnerable they have survived as a species through their ability to solve the problems through skilful thinking. One way to strengthen problem-solving skills, and to encourage skilful and flexible thinking, is to engage in thinking games and simulations that pose problems and provide challenges that exercise and extend thinking. The following games can be played, adapted or extended to provide problem-solving challenges for players of all ages.

## Problem solver

In this game players are presented with a problem-solving challenge, and must try to create the best solution to a design brief within a given time.

*Players*:      Any number, playing individually, in pairs or small team groups

*Age range*:   Seven to adult

*Materials*:    Pen/pencil and sketch paper, plus large sheets of paper for finished designs

*How to play*

Two or more teams are given a problem which they try to solve, and must present their solution in a drawing or design that makes their solution visible to others. These problem-solving designs are assessed by other players who must judge which design they think presents the best solution to the problem. The design judged to be best wins the game.

Suitable design challenges must be prepared before the game. Some intriguing creative thinking problems can be found in Edward de Bono's book *Children Solve Problems*, for example to design:

- a dog-exercising machine
- a machine to weigh an elephant
- ways to improve the human body
- a method to prevent a dog and cat fighting
- a sleep machine

Other design topics include:

- a machine to cut hair
- a machine to dig tunnels
- a fruit picking machine
- a money (or egg) sorting machine
- a secret den or hideaway
- a pet's home
- a device for watering plants while you are away
- a bird scarer
- a climbing frame
- a litter bin

The game can be played by individual players, pairs or group teams as follows:

1  Two or more teams are given the same problem to solve. They must present their chosen solution in a labelled drawing by the end of a given time period eg thirty minutes.

2  Teams may not see what solutions other teams are working on.

3  When the time is up each team presents their solution to a panel of judges who have not been involved in this design problem. The judges can ask questions of each team, if they wish, about the solutions presented. The judges choose the winning design.

Teams can play in one Design-a-solution game and then act as judges of another game going on in the same class, which means that all players can be involved in both the design and the judging process. It is helpful for the judges to be asked to identify at least one good aspect of each design, and to say what criteria they have used in selecting the winning design. Joint winners are allowed.

*Questions to think about*

- What kind of problem were you asked to solve?

- Was there only one solution or many to the problem?

- Is there ever only one answer to a problem? Can you give an example?

- Does every problem have an answer? Can you give an example of a problem without an answer?

- Do you prefer to work out solutions to problems by yourself or with others? What problems, when and why?

- Do you think there is always a best solution to a problem?

- Is it easier to talk about a solution, or to show it in a drawing? Why is this? Can you give an example?

- Could you identify something good in every solution?

- Is it fair that there should be a winner in this game? Was the competition fair?

- What problem would you most like to see solved? How might it be solved?

*Extension activities*

Collect problems for discussion or to use in playing this game, for example by having a problem box or board in a public place for all to contribute to.

Investigate today's newspaper. What problems can be found?

## Radar

This one of a family of games which rely on a group guiding one of their blindfold members through a problem-solving route to a winning point. Such games require planning, spatial thinking and communication skills. The following version is suitable for younger players.

*Players*:       Three or more, playing in teams or as a group

*Age range*:    Five to adult

*Materials*:     Chalk and chalkboard, or pen and whiteboard/large sheet of paper. Blindfold or large paper bag

## How to play

A player is blindfolded, or has a large paper bag put over their head, and uses information from other players to try to draw a line to a small circle drawn on a chalkboard, whiteboard or large piece of paper.

1   A player is chosen, is blindfolded and is led to a large board (and given a piece of chalk or pen to write with).

2   One of the other players draws a small circle anywhere on the board, keeping it secret from the blindfolded player.

3   The blindfolded player draws a line on the board and tries to reach the circle that has been drawn.

4   The other players guide the blindfolded player by giving 'radar' bleeps, beeping slowly when the line is far from the circle and faster when the line comes nearer the circle.

5   When the circle is reached the game ends. The blindfolded player chooses the next person to play, or a player from the next team has a turn.

Before playing the game for the first time players may need practice in making slow or fast beeping noises at the right time. Remind players that their beeps should become faster (or slower) rather than louder. Players or teams can be timed to see who is the fastest to reach the circle.

## Questions to think about

• This game is called 'radar'. What is 'radar'?

• Did you think this was a good game to play? Why?

• In what ways is being blindfolded like or unlike being blind?

• What do people who are blind, or blindfolded, have to think about which sighted people do not?

• Which is the most important ability to have – sight, speech or hearing? Which would you least like to lose?

- Was playing Radar easy or difficult? Why?

- Have you ever lost your way? What happened? What should (or could) you have done?

*Extension activities*

Invent your own variation of the game of Radar, or try a harder version such as 'North, south, east and west' (below).

Research what radar is, when it was invented and why it was and is so useful.

Investigate how blind animals such as bats avoid bumping into things.

Find out how blind people navigate their world. Experiment by having one child blindfolded and put under the protection and guidance of a partner, then reverse roles.

Visit a flight control centre at an airport, or interview a pilot to find out more about modern navigation methods.


## North, south, east and west

This is a challenging navigation game in which a player must try to reach a point of safety by finding a route through an obstacle course while blindfolded, helped by instructions from other players. This game exercises forward planning, spatial thinking and communication skills.

*Players*:      Any number, playing in pairs or groups

*Age range*:    Seven to adult

*Materials*:    A number of 'obstacles' such as chairs, waste paper baskets etc.

*How to play*

Players are split into two teams, or play as one group. One player is blindfolded eg with a large paper bag over their head, and must navigate an obstacle course from one side of the room to another, with the help of information given by other players in the group or team. The player wins by reaching the other side safely without touching any obstacle (or as few as possible).

1   A player goes to one end of the room and is blindfolded.

2   Other players, or members of the other team, re-arrange any of the

furniture or other objects in the room to make it difficult to cross. A clear route (eg one metre wide) must be left for the blindfold player to move through to 'safety' on the opposite side of the room.

3 The blindfold player must try to find a route to the opposite side of the room without touching any objects.

4 Other players can help by giving information on which way to go eg 'right, left, forward, back' or points of the compass eg 'north, south, east, west etc.'

5 When the player reaches 'safety' at the other end of the room, or gives up, the game ends. Players getting there by touching the fewest number of obstacles, or in the shortest time, win.

*Questions to think about*

- What makes this game difficult to play if you are blindfolded?

- Is it easy or difficult giving a blindfold player directions? Why is this?

- Would you get better at this game with practice? Why?

- Is this game like life, or like anything in your life? If so, in what ways?

- Is there any benefit in playing this game. Why, or why not?

- Does every problem have some objective to reach?

- Does every problem have some obstacle to overcome?

- Can you think of a problem with an objective and an obstacle (or obstacles)?

- Do you have any objective you want to reach in your own life? Are there any obstacles in your way? What are they? How could you achieve your object or overcome the obstacles?

- What advice would you give to someone who told you they had a problem?

*Extension activities*

Invent your own 'obstacle' game?

Draw a map of life showing some of the obstacles and objectives.

Discuss a book or story. Try to identify the objectives that the characters are seeking, and the obstacles that they have to overcome.

## Steps

In this game players estimate the movements required to reach a goal. The game involves practice in estimating, planning, testing hypotheses and creative thinking.

*Players:*       Any number, playing individually or in teams

*Age range:*   Seven to adult

*Materials:*    Pen/pencil and paper, and a long space to play in.

### How to play

Each player devises a way of moving towards a goal, and estimates how many of those moves it will take to reach the goal. The winner is the player who reaches the goal, or nearest to the goal, in their estimated number of moves. This game can be played individually, or in two teams.

1   A player is chosen as scorekeeper for the game. A line is drawn or made in front of the players as a starting point. The scorekeeper chooses a goal about 25–30 feet away from the starting line, for example a tree or the opposite wall of a room.

2   The first player tells the others the type of movement chosen, and the number of moves it will take to reach the goal. For example: ' I am twelve giant steps from the goal', 'I am fifteen hops from the goal', I am  thirty pigeon steps from the goal' or 'I am five hops, six skips and three jumps from the goal'.

3   The player must show the others an example of the move before starting. This will be helpful if an odd or unknown movement is chosen like a 'squiggle' or 'swivel step'. Other players are asked to estimate, and say or record, whether the player's estimated number of movements is too high, too low or just right.

4   The player then tries to prove the estimate by moving from the starting point to the goal in the stated number of moves. The other players count the number of moves being taken.

5   If the goal is reached in the estimated number of moves the player, and those thinking his estimate was right, win. If the goal was reached too soon, those who thought the estimate too high win. If the goal was not reached in the stated number of moves, those who thought the estimate low win.

6   Each player has a turn in estimating and trying to prove it right.

Remember that each player's plan for reaching the goal must be different from those of all the previous players.

7   When all players have had a turn the number of correct judgements are added and the individual or team with the highest score wins.

Another way of scoring is to give a point for each move above or below the estimated number to the other players or to the opposing team. If for example the player estimates two hops and twelve jumps, but takes three jumps more the other players get three points. If the player gets there in ten instead of twelve jumps they get 12–10 = two points.

*Questions to think about*

• What does 'estimation' mean?

Which movements was it most easy and most difficult to estimate?

Were you successful in your estimates? Why was this?

Which was the most interesting movement chosen in the game? Why do you think so?

• Were you accurate in estimating your own movement? Why was this?

• Why do you think this game is called 'Steps'? Can you think of a better title for this game?

• When might you have to estimate things in your life?

• Are you good at estimating things? Can you give an example?

• The Chinese have a saying: 'A journey of a thousand miles begins with one step.' What do you think they mean by this?

• The Greek philosopher Heraclitus said 'You cannot step into the same river twice.' What do you think he meant by this? Do you agree with him?

*Extension activities*

Brainstorm as many different ways as you can think of for moving from the start to the goal.

Play the estimation game in recording personal athletic records eg long jump, high jump, hop-step-and-jump, standing jump, putting the shot, throwing a ball and so on.

Create your own estimation game.

Play other estimation games, see Estimation p 99.

# Index of games

# Afterword

This book contains over 120 games for thinking that have been played successfully with children, but there must be many more games that work just as well in providing challenge and entertainment to players of all ages. If you have a thinking game to share please contact:

Dr. Robert Fisher
Brunel University
300 St. Margaret's Road,
Twickenham TW1 1PT